PROTESTANTISM
in Central America

WILTON M. NELSON

WILLIAM B. EERDMANS PUBLISHING COMPANY
GRAND RAPIDS, MICHIGAN

Copyright ©1984 by Wm. B. Eerdmans Publishing
Company
255 Jefferson Ave. S.E., Grand Rapids, Michigan 49503

Translated from the Spanish edition, *El Protestantismo en
Centro América,* ©1982 Editorial Caribe, San José, Costa
Rica

**Library of Congress Cataloging in Publication
Data**

Nelson, Wilton M.
  Protestantism in Central America.

  Translation of El Protestantismo en Centro América.
  1. Protestant churches—Central America—History.
2. Central America—Church history. I. Title.
BX4833.5.N4413 1984   280.4'098   84-13727

ISBN 0-8028-0024-6 (pbk.)

Bookstore

3 04

Contents

8 Dec. 84

69899

Preface

This book was originally written in Spanish at the invitation of the Commission for Studies of the History of the Church in Latin America (CEHILA), a group of Roman Catholic historians whose purpose was to compile a definitive history of Christianity in this part of the world. When completed, their efforts will result in eight or nine volumes. The Commission revealed a finesse and ecumenical spirit in inviting the cooperation of Protestant historians.

Middle and South America was divided into seven areas (the eighth includes Hispanics in the United States and Canada), with representatives, both Protestant and Catholic, chosen for each area. The present writer was named as the Protestant representative of Central America.

Being an enthusiast regarding the church history of the land where I have lived and labored forty-four years, I immediately began to work on the assignment, finishing it in 1975—long before the publication date of the *magnum opus* sponsored by CEHILA. As I desired to share the results of my investigation with evangelical brethren and others as soon as possible, I asked CEHILA for permission to publish the contribution ahead of time; the Commission very kindly granted my request.

Given the fact that today the eyes of the world are more than ever on these overlooked and neglected countries, Wm. B. Eerdmans Publishing Company asked me to put this brief history of Protestantism in Central America into English, and encouraged me to add an appendix updating the history to the present.

I must call the reader's attention to the brevity of this work, which is due to the fact that Protestant history is recent in comparison with the centuries of Roman Catholicism, and evangelicals are still a small—though rapidly growing—minority. (When the original work was written in 1974 the evangelical community composed only 5 percent of the area's population. In 1980 it had risen to 10 percent.) Therefore the portion corresponding to Protestantism must of necessity be small in the total history of Christianity in Latin America. Because of this brevity many important and interesting aspects of Protestant history in the Central American isthmus are missing. Many groups and persons who have realized praiseworthy works are not even mentioned, which is lamentable but unavoidable, and we hope it will be understood.

WILTON M. NELSON

San Jose, Costa Rica
November 1983

I

Protestantism During the Colonial Era

An interesting and important historical coincidence is the fact that the conquest of the Americas and the Protestant Reformation were contemporary events. Hernán Cortés was born in 1485 and Martin Luther in 1483; the former died in 1547 and the latter in 1546. The conquest of Mexico began in 1519, just two years after Luther nailed his 95 theses on the door of the Castle Church in Wittenberg. During the years of the conquest of Mexico (1519–21) Luther wrote the famous tracts that were to become the groundwork of Protestant theology and the cause of his excommunication. The year in which the conquest was completed (1521) was also the year of the famous Diet of Worms.

When studying the history of Protestantism in Latin America, it is important to remember that, during the period immediately preceding the Reformation, the Spaniards became the most militant defenders of Roman Catholicism. This was due in large measure to their centuries-long struggle for freedom from the Moslem Moors, during which they became extremely fervent Roman Catholics. The Spaniards, under Ferdinand and Isabel, won complete liberation from this politico-religious domination in 1492, the same year in which Columbus, under the auspices of these sovereigns, discovered the Americas.

Twenty-five years later another threat to the Church of Rome arose: the Protestant Reformation. Spain, which had become the champion of the Church, came to her defense as no other nation and became the worst enemy of the Reformation. Spanish Catholicism produced the Jesuit Order whose theologians dominated the Council of Trent and gave Roman Catholic theology a totally anti-Protestant interpretation. The Spanish Inquisition, the cruelest and most efficient form of this institution, was extended to all the colonies of the immense Spanish Empire. Under such circumstances it was extremely difficult for Protestantism to penetrate this part of the world.

On the other hand, England, which became the bulwark of the Protestant Reformation, rivaled Spain in the domination of the New World. Pirates (such as Drake, Hawkins, and Morgan) mercilessly harassed the commerce between Spain and her colonies. In 1585 Drake captured the sea ports of Santo Domingo and Cartagena (which, however, were later recovered). In the next century England captured and retained various Spanish islands. In 1655, during the era of Cromwell, Jamaica was taken. Roman Catholicism was proscribed and Anglicanism was established on the island.[1] More islands were taken over and in the eighteenth century Trinidad was captured. As a result, Protestantism in various forms was introduced in the West Indies.

The British, not satisfied with the possession of a number of West Indian islands, also invaded the Atlantic coast of Central America. In 1638 several shipwrecked Englishmen (one source calls them "Buccaneers")[2] settled in a place later called Belize. The colony grew, following the capture of Jamaica, until in 1670 it had 700 inhabitants and prospered with the exploitation of precious woods such as logwood and later mahogany. The Spaniards tried to recapture "British Honduras" but were unsuccessful.[3] Under British protection, Belize became a Protestant enclave in Central America, and in the nineteenth century it was a source of Protestant pioneer missionary work.

The British extended their influence and dominion to the northern coast of Honduras where, from 1642 on, they occupied the Bay Islands. Beginning in 1678 they also assumed a protectorate over the kingdom of the Miskito Indians, who lived on what is now the eastern coast of Nicaragua.

Thus, the British controlled in varying degrees all the Atlantic coast of Central America, from Belize in the north to Greytown (San Juan del Norte) in the south. This hegemony continued even after Central America gained its independence. However, before the end of the nineteenth century England's political domination ended (with the exception of British Honduras),[4] although the religious and cultural influence of the British along the coast continues to this day. In sum, due to the British domination of the Caribbean coasts, Protestantism penetrated Central America even during its colonial period.

Throughout this era, pirates and buccaneers had hideouts in such places as Belize, Roatan, and Bluefields, from which they stole away to attack and loot

the Spanish galleons loaded with silver and gold—
which the Spaniards in turn had taken from the Indians. It is quite evident that all of the pirates were
Protestants, if they made any profession at all, and it is
curious to note that they gave a religious interpretation
to their activities. According to Stephen Caiger, an
Anglican priest in Belize, "they looked upon the plun-
dering of the Spanish as almost a Holy War against the
greed of the *conquistadores* and the cruelty of the
Inquisition. . . . Every ship had its Bible on which the
Oath of Brotherhood was sworn."[5]

Logwood settlements arose along the shores from
the Campeche Bay in Mexico to the Miskito Coast in
Nicaragua. Therefore, says Caiger, "it is likely that the
[Anglican] Church very soon had established herself
[among them] in one form or another."[6] The work of
the Anglicans took on a missionary character. The
Society for the Propagation of the Gospel named Na-
than Price as its first missionary in this area. Price
"ministered to the Miskito Indians, then under British
protectorate, and died in the famous pirate island of
Roatan."[7]

In 1815 the Anglican Cathedral of St. John the
Baptist was constructed in Belize. Its archives contain
the records of the coronation in 1845 of Frederick, the
king of the Miskito Coast, and the baptism and con-
firmtion of the heir apparent a few years later.[8]

It should be recognized that the Protestantism
described above was something that developed entirely
apart from the life of the Spanish-American colonies.
This was due in part to the fact that the Spaniards
usually settled in the more healthful highlands of the
interior and some on the Pacific coast, staying away

from the hot, humid, disease-infected regions of the Atlantic coast. This made it easier for the British domination of the area and the extension of Protestantism, a proscribed religion in the Spanish colonies. However, the archives of the Inquisitional Tribunals indicate that individual Protestants did live in the lands under direct control of Spain.

The Inquisition had existed in Spanish America almost from the beginning of the conquest, but only as an episcopal institution;[9] not until 1569 was it established as an arm of the Spanish Empire (the "Spanish Inquisition"), when Phillip II on January 25 issued a *cédula* ordering the establishment of tribunals in Lima and Mexico City. In 1610 a third tribunal was set up in Cartagena, Columbia.

In addition to these principal tribunals there were inferior branches called *comisarías*. The chief one in Central America was established in Guatemala City toward the end of 1572.[10] However, many other *comisarías*, apparently subordinate to that in Guatemala City, were found throughout the isthmus, at Acajutla, Cartago, Ciudad Real, Chiapas de los Indios, Chiquimula, Corpus, Escuintla, Gracias a Dios, Huehuetenango, Jalapa, León, Los Llanos (Sa Bartolóme), Metapas, Nicoya, Nueva Segovia, Ocosuntepeque, Olancho, Quetzaltenango, Quezaylica, Realejo, Santa Ana Grande, San Antonio Suchitepéquez, San Miguel, San Salvador, Santo Tomás, San Vincente, Soconuso, Sololá, Sonsonate, Suchitepéquez, Tegucigalpa, Tila, Totonicapán, Tuxtla, Verapaz, Zacapa, and Zapotitlán.[11]

What provoked the establishment of these tribunals and this network of *comisarías*? It was precisely the fear of the penetration of Protestantism in the colonies, as the Guatemalan authority on this subject, Ernesto Chinchilla Aguilar, affirms:

> The persecution of Protestants constitutes one of the principal activities of the Holy Office in America . . . especially in the part that we are studying [Central America], the persecution of Protestants constitutes, not the most quantitative aspect of the inquisitorial activity, but indeed the most substantive and principal object of the Holy Office.
>
> Not the unbelieving Moors and Jews of the [Iberian] Peninsula, nor the unbelieving native Americans nor the unbelieving Asiatics of the Philippines moved the Spanish Crown to establish the Inquisition in the Americas, but rather the appearance of the [Protestant] Reformation in the center of Europe and . . . in England. . . .
>
> During the reign of Charles I [V], but more frequently in that of Phillip II, the Crown urged the civil authorities and the American bishops to zealously persecute every outbreak of Protestantism. . . . there came a time when so great was the number of ships and corsairs in the waters of the New World, and so many Protestants that were able to settle on American soil that with reason the term "heretic" supplanted in ordinary language the word "infidel," the common word during the first years of the colony. . . .
>
> Thus it is not strange that in the *Capitanía* of Guatemala, from the middle of the sixteenth century on, the bishops with special instruction from the Crown deal with cases of Lutherans, in their capacity as apostolic inquisitors.[12]

However, in reality there were few concrete cases of Protestantism in the colonies, although there were many suspects. The first case in Central America was a Greek carpenter named Francisco. He was denounced as a Lutheran in Granada, Nicaragua, in 1556. But in 1562 Bishop Carrasco freed him as one who had been "reconciled" (to the church) in the *auto de fe* (the religious ceremony in which sentences of the tribunals were announced) of January 1562.[13] The second case was Nicolás de Sanctour, a Frenchman accused of Lutheranism and processed in Comayagua, Honduras, in 1560. It is said that he was "reconciled" in May of 1562.[14] Another was Charles de Salgante, also a Frenchman, processed for Lutheranism in Trujillo, Honduras, in 1560 but "reconciled" the following year.[15]

In 1564 Phillip II issued a special *cédula* "urging particularly the bishop of Nicaragua to pursue zealously the disciples of Luther in his diocese." Chinchilla Aguilar conjectures that the cases just mentioned produced so great a concern that the king issued this *cédula.*[16]

After the establishment of the Spanish Inquisition more presumed cases of Lutheranism are registered. Peter Jones, an Englishman, was tried in Honduras, 1572;[17] Jerónimo Monto from Milan was judged in Soconusco three times but absolved in 1590 in Mexico because he "was tormented and gave up."[18]

In the same epoch there were two other important cases in Nicaragua: in Granada the case of Enrique, a Flemish tailor accused of Lutheranism, and in Realejo a carpenter, Simón, who was denounced for having spoken against the religious *fiestas* and for sustaining correspondence with English pirates.[19] In the sixteenth century there was a total of twenty-one accusations and reports of Protestantism in Central America.[20]

In the seventeenth century the number of trials for Protestantism decreased. During the first half of the century only five cases were given consideration, and none in the last half, although there were a few accusations.[21] Therefore it is clear that in Central America during the colonial era ecclesiastical Protestantism existed only in lands under British domination. In the Spanish colonies the only kind of Protestantism to be found was that of a few cases of individuals whose faith was of little depth, since under torture and the threat of death almost all denied or renounced it.

According to available data, only one of the Protestants apprehended by the Inquisition in Central America was ready to die for his faith. John Martin (alias "William Cornelius") was a member of a pirate expedition, led by the famous John Hawkins, that ended in shipwreck on the coast of Campeche (Mexico) in 1568. He settled in Guatemala where he practiced the professions of barber and surgeon. In 1574 he was apprehended and sent to the tribunal in Mexico. Refusing to renounce his Protestant faith, he was condemned to *relajación*. He was hanged and given over to be burned in the *quemadero* located in the San Hipólito Market, near the streets of Badillo and Colón in the Mexico City of today.[22]

It would appear that the Inquisition realized its purpose: it freed the colonies from the threat of Protestantism. As a result there was a complete "blackout" of the Protestant faith until the time of the independence movement.

II

Protestantism During the Nineteenth Century

We have seen that during the colonial era doors were hermetically sealed to Protestantism in Central America. It was a criminal offense to be a Protestant and the Holy Inquisition constituted the secret police to watch that none entered and to expel or execute any who did slip in.

Due to the intimate union of church and state, the Inquisition had a political as well as religious character. It was not only the "Inquisition" but also "Spanish." Some modern apologists for the Roman Catholic Church, in order to free her from guilt for the existence of this horrible institution, insist that it was chiefly a state institution. We shall not here discuss the matter as to which was the most responsible, yet it must be admitted that there was a political aspect to the Inquisition. Therefore, when independence from Spain was won, the Spanish Inquisition, which was one of the aspects of Spanish domination most hated by the patriots, disappeared.[1] So the independence movement removed the greatest obstacle for the entrance of Protestants.

Political independence did not come spontaneously. Rather, it was the product of a number of factors. Among them was the clandestine penetration of the philosophy of the "Enlightenment" (the movement that produced the French Revolution), especially its concept of the "Rights of Man," among which were the right of people to choose their own government, the freedom of conscience, and the freedom of religion. It should be pointed out, however, that the main interest of the Spanish Americans was political and commercial liberty and not religious freedom. But the very idea of "liberty" included a religious aspect. This of course was vitally related to the entrance of Protestantism in Central America.

Here, as in the rest of Spanish America, the hierarchy opposed the independence movement. In Guatemala, Archbishop Casus y Torres, who was enthroned in 1811, thundered from his pulpit against the independence movement. In 1829 (Guatemala having declared her independence in 1821), he was banished to Cuba, accused of participating in a plot against the new government.[2]

On the other hand, many of the lower clergy favored independence. In Guatemala one of the first to spread propaganda in favor of political freedom was the canon doctor José María Castillo. The "Tertulia Política" ("Patriotic Club"), a group influenced by the Enlightenment philosophy that had penetrated the colony in spite of the vigilance of the Inquisitors, held its meetings in his home.[3] In El Salvador, where the first cry for independence in Central America was heard, Presbyter José Matías Delgado not only advocated independence but also promoted a conspiracy in its favor in November 1811.[4] When at last Central America declared its independence on September 15, 1821, thirteen of the twenty-nine persons who signed the document were priests.[5]

However, one must not conclude that religious liberty came automatically with independence. To the contrary, the article on religion in the new Constitution, elaborated by the Constituent Assembly of the Federal Republic of Central America in 1824, read as follows: "Her religion is the Roman Catholic Apostolic with the exclusion of the public exercise of any other."[6] The Central Americans had no complaint with Roman Catholicism as such (save with some of its hierarchs). Instead, they sought backing from the church.

The contribution of independence to the growth of Protestantism was more indirect than direct. Under colonial paternalism Spanish Americans were prohibited contact with countries other than Spain. With the independence these restrictions were gone and the new nations exposed to all the currents of modern life. They soon began to have commercial relations with Protestant nations. For example, in 1843 Captain William Le Lacheur, a fervent Protestant Englishman, took the first shipload of Costa Rican coffee to London and established a relationship with England that was the main factor in lifting Costa Rica out of the extreme poverty and backwardness that had characterized her during the colonial period.[7]

The Central American provinces were extremely

backward in every sense at the end of the colonial era. In Costa Rica "during the first years of the nineteenth century you could count with the fingers of one hand the number of schools *de primeras letras* [lit. "of first letters"]. Very few people could read or write."[8] Through contact with the rest of the world, the leaders of the new nations became conscious of their backwardness. Furthermore, they saw the Protestant countries were the most progressive and advanced of the time (e.g., Great Britain, Germany, Holland, Switzerland, the Scandinavian countries, and the United States of America). In many of the new Latin American countries the idea arose that one way to elevate their cultural and economic level would be to promote the immigration of peoples from these countries. Juan Bautista Alberdi, statesman in the newly liberated but backward and sparsely populated Republic of Argentina, declared as axiomatic *"gobernar es poblar"* ("to govern is to populate") and *"libertad religiosa es el medio de poblar"* ("religious liberty is the means of populating").[9] Some Central American politicians agreed with Alberdi.

But here was a problem: the Constitution of Central America prohibited the public exercise of any non-Catholic worship. How could Protestants be invited to immigrate to lands where the practice of their faith would be prohibited? Costa Rican leaders became aware of this anomaly. In 1852 some in the progressive administration of Juan Rafael Mora (1849–59) were saying:

> Our primary need is the immigration of foreigners . . . without them we shall vegetate for a

century in status quo.... But the foreigner, before coming to our shores has his fears....

So then the first conditions for immigration are: freedom to work, freedom of industry, civil liberty, *freedom of worship* [italics mine]....

But European emigration does not turn to the Spanish American Republics, because it does not find in them any of these advantages for its moral and material life which the Northland [USA] offers.

We need immigration at all costs and if we really wish to get out of the state of semibarbarism, if we wish to get out of the rut and enter fully into the way of progress, if we wish to get rid of our problems and ignorance, we must hurry and share with North America the guarantees granted to the foreigner....

Let us assure the foreigner the observance of his beliefs in the freedom of worship, the freedom of his heart to choose a wife [10]

The obstacles to Protestant immigration began to be removed first of all by means of clauses in treaties of friendship and commerce with Protestant nations, which granted religious liberty to the citizens of the contracting nations (e.g., Costa Rica with Germany in 1848, with Great Britain in 1849, and with the USA in 1851). Later, religious liberty began to appear in the constitutions themselves, first in the form of tolerance (tacit or explicit) and finally in the form of complete liberty.

The Republic of Central America was formed in a conservative atmosphere, which explains the tenor of the article in the Constitution of 1824 prohibiting the public exercise of any non-Catholic worship. But in

1829 the liberals took over the government and initiated drastic reforms. Among them was a decree in 1832
regarding religious liberty that afterward was incorporated into the Constitution of 1835. It read as follows:

> The inhabitants of the Republic may worship
> God according to the dictates of their conscience.
> The government [of the Republic] will protect
> them in their freedom of worship. However, the
> States shall look after the prevalent religion of its
> people and maintain all worship [*todo culto*] in
> harmony with the law.[11]

This law was practically annulled during the conservative epoch of Rafael Carrera (1839–65) in Guatemala. Nevertheless, the desire for European
immigration always remained. The Carrera regime was
overthrown and the liberals took over with more zeal
than ever. Religious liberty was restored in 1873 by the
administration of Justo Rufino Barrios who believed
that "such liberty would help to attract immigrants to
Guatemala."[12]

In the same year Barrios decreed the validity of
the marriage of foreigners performed in accord with a
religion different from the dominant religion of the
Republic. He believed that this also would help promote immigration.[13]

One must not imagine that this religious liberty
provoked a missionary campaign (see pp. 30ff.). But it is
true that at mid-century some Protestant immigrants
did come to central America—especially British and
Germans. The political conditions in continental Eu-
rope, resulting from the 1848 revolution, caused some
Germans to look to Costa Rica as a place of refuge.[14]

Later on in the century a few Swiss came to Costa Rica as well.[15]

In this era, properly speaking, it was not Protestantism that came—merely Protestants. They came not as propagandists of their religion but as immigrants whose religion was Protestantism. Nevertheless, they suffered difficulties in their new environment. This is not surprising when one realizes that these countries had been under the dominion of Spanish Roman Catholicism for three and a half centuries. According to Moritz Wagner and Karl Scherzer, Germans who visited Costa Rica in 1852 and 1853,

> The people at times honor the Protestants with the slanderous nickname of *machos* ("mules"), because they consider them as animals in regard to religion. Apart from this there is no aversion to the Protestants. However, a non-Catholic, who wishes to marry a daughter of the country, must become a Catholic, be rebaptized and sprinkled with a considerable amount of holy water to rid him of all heresy.[16]

One of the chief difficulties that Protestants ran into was what to do with those of their number who died. Until 1884 all cemeteries in Costa Rica belonged to the Church of Rome, which would not permit the burial of heretics in its graveyards. In 1850, after several shameful incidents in relation to the death of various dissidents, the government granted the Protestants a small property near the General Cemetery where they might bury their dead. In 1884 all cemeteries were secularized and thus the problem disappeared.[17]

By 1864, in spite of the vexations suffered, there were 286 Protestants in Costa Rica, which had a total

population in that year of 120,499.[18] Not many, however, showed any fervor or enthusiasm about their
faith. It would appear that most of them at best were
nominal and not practicing Protestants, especially the
Germans, among whom were some disposed to aban-
don their faith in order to marry Costa Rican *señoritas.*
According to Wagner and Scherzer,

> A number of Germans, whom the priest would
> not marry, because they were Protestants, to
> daughters of the land, became Catholics in secret.
> But Dr. S. did it publicly and with considerable
> ostentation. It is said that he stood barefoot and
> dressed in a grey shirt of penitence at the en-
> trance of the cathedral in Cartago. The venerable
> clergy sprinkled him with holy water and applied
> incense profusely to remove from him all rem-
> nants of heresy.[19]

The British showed more interest in practicing
their faith. About the year 1848 the previously mentioned British sea captain, William Le Lacheur, obtained permission from the Costa Rican government
for Protestant public worship.[20] During the first seventeen years the services were held in private homes. The
first Protestant chapel was built in 1865; it was called
the "Iron Church" since it was a prefabricated structure
made of iron. The pieces were brought to Costa Rica
in Captain Le Lacheur's ships. During this era the British Empire was expanding rapidly and most likely the
government of Her Majesty Queen Victoria sponsored
the manufacture of such chapels as part of its expan-
sionist policy.[21] (The true name of the church was "The
Church of the Good Shepherd," and so it remains to
this day.)

Until 1869 the congregation had no ordained minister, and laymen officiated in the services. The first pastor was Dr. Richard Brealey, a fervent Christian layman as well as physician. Occasionally the British Consul officiated. At one time it was Richard Farrer, the same man who constructed the first railroad in Costa Rica, the exotic *Burrocarril.*[22]

In the beginning the church had an interdenominational character. The first ordained ministers were Congregationalists and Methodists. But with the passing of time the worship service took on a more Anglican character until in 1896 it was incorporated into the diocese of Belize and remained under this jurisdiction until 1947, when it was transferred to the Episcopal Church of the USA, becoming a part of the Episcopal Missionary District of the Panama Canal Zone.[23] In 1956 Central America was converted into a separate missionary diocese and in 1968 each Central American republic was constituted a diocese.

It has been said that the Church of the Good Shepherd "was the first place of public Protestant worship in the Central American Republics." This may be true if one uses the term "Central America" in the old political sense, but it is definitely not so if it is used geographically. Fifty years earlier (1815), St. John's Cathedral (Anglican) had been built in Belize, British Honduras, which forms part of Central America. During the nineteenth century, and even before, Anglicanism had been extended within and outside of the colony.

In 1822 the British Baptists began work in Belize and in 1835 built their first chapel.[24] Their work continues to this day.

Since 1825 the Methodists have labored in Brit-

ish Honduras.²⁵ The northern coast of Honduras and
the Bay Islands were under British dominion for almost
the entire colonial era, and it was not until 1859 that
they became a part of the Republic. Therefore Protestantism predominated there, especially Methodism.²⁶

Along the eastern coast of Nicaragua there arose
a strong Protestantism among the British, negroes, and
Indians who inhabited the area. Anglicans had shown
some concern for the Miskito Indians during the seventeenth century but produced no permanent work
among them. However, at the middle of the nineteenth
century the Moravian Church (descendent of the fif-
teenth-century Hussite movement, with its center now
in Herrnhut, Saxony, Germany), possessed by missionary zeal, began a notable work in this area. The center
of its activity was Bluefields, which was also an important base for the British domination of the area. The
Moravian mission was initiated in the following manner:

The Miskito Indians shared the British enmity
toward the Spaniards. This united them in a political
friendship, and in 1670 a Miskito kingdom was formed
under the protectorate of Great Britian. The Indian
king admired everything that was British. To show his
appreciation for two Englishmen and also to promote
British immigration, the king gave them 108 square
miles of his kingdom. The gift did not interest the
Englishmen but they accepted it so as not to offend the
king. They tried to sell it to a German prince named
Schönberg, a friend of the Moravians. Schönberg, before
making the purchase, ordered an investigation. Those
who reconnoitered the land brought him not only a
report concerning the terrain but also an account of
the tragic conditions in which the natives were living.

The result was an urgent appeal on the part of the prince to Herrnhut for missionaries to the Miskitos. The Moravians accepted the challenge. In 1849 the first missionaries arrived at Bluefields, where they were well received by the British consul as well as by the Miskito king, George August Frederick.[27]

Thus was born the Moravian Church in Central America, which in 1973 had 32,177 adherents in Nicaragua and 4,566 in Honduras.[28] The Moravians have done a notable work, social and cultural as well as ecclesiastical. But here again it must be pointed out that this work was begun not among Latins but rather among Indians, Africans, British, and mixed elements ("Creoles") of these races.

To the south of Bluefields, on the same coast, was a port called San Juan del Norte, located at the mouth of the important navigable San Juan River. In 1848 the British seized the port and named it "Greytown." (It was returned to Nicaragua in 1860.) The German explorers Wagner and Scherzer, in their trip to Costa Rica (1852, 1853), noted that there was in Greytown an "English Protestant Church."[29]

The coming of foreigners to Panama and Costa Rica during the last half of the nineteenth century caused the establishment of more Protestant churches in Central America.

There had always been much traffic across the Isthmus of Panama, but this was greatly increased by the discovery of gold in California (1849). To facilitate the traffic a railroad was constructed across the isthmus (completed in 1855). It was built by North Americans, which meant the arrival of many Protestants. By 1849, according to the Panamanian newspaper *The Star,*

Sunday worship services with Episcopalian liturgy were being held in a hotel.[30] In 1853 the Episcopal Church began formal work in Panama. In 1864 the Railroad Company built "Christ Church by the Sea."[31]

During the last decades of the nineteenth century huge enterprises attracted many non-Catholics: the De Lesseps project to dig a canal across Panama (1879–88); the construction of a railroad from Port Limón to San José in Costa Rica (1873–90); and the contemporary beginning of the banana industry on the Atlantic coast of Costa Rica. French, British, North Americans and especially West Indians came to Panama and Costa Rica.

The heavy affluence of West Indians was due to the fact that these enterprises were developed in the hot and humid coastal lowlands, where deadly tropical diseases abounded (malaria, yellow fever, and blackwater fever), and white Europeans succumbed easily to them. (The remedies that in recent years have successfully combatted these dread diseases had not yet been discovered). Mortality rates were frightfully high among the whites who came to work in these areas. Consequently, to get this work done it was necessary to import negroes from the West Indies, who possessed more immunity to these diseases. Hundreds of them came, especially from Jamaica.

During the nineteenth century Jamaica was almost entirely Protestant. When England conquered the island in 1655, the practice of Roman Catholicism was prohibited and the prohibition was not removed until 1792.[32] Also at this time arose a fervent Protestantism due to a notable revival.[33] Therefore, on coming to these new lands the Jamaicans soon manifested their desire for public worship. The Methodists and the Baptists revealed the most fervor. By 1884 there was a Methodist missionary in Panama,[34] and the Baptists had organized a church in Port Limón, Costa Rica, as did the Methodists in 1894 and the Anglicans in 1896.[35]

All this meant a considerable increase in the Protestant population of Central America. In 1878 some Capuchin missionaries visited Port Limón and reported that in the city were more Protestants than Catholics and not even a small meeting place (*ermita*) for the latter could be found.[36] The Protestant population in Costa Rica increased from 268 in 1864 to 1,392 in 1883 and to 2,245 in 1892, according to the census taken in those years.[37]

It should be understood that this increase was not due to the conversion of native Central Americans but rather to the influx of foreigners. It was not until 1882 in Guatemala and 1891 in Costa Rica that the first Protestant missionaries came with the purpose of working among Latin Americans. Furthermore, during the first years of the ministry of these missionaries, conversions were few.

In view of the above, the Protestantism of the nineteenth century in Central America must be called "Foreign Protestantism."

III

The Beginnings
of National Protestantism

Background

It was not until the end of the nineteenth century that Protestantism began to penetrate among the Spanish-American peoples of Central America. There were reasons for this delay; first, Protestants in general, with a few exceptions, revealed little interest in missions until the beginning of the nineteenth century. Moreover, when they did awaken to their missionary responsibility, very few considered Latin America a legitimate mission field. As we have seen, the Anglicans in the eighteenth century and the Moravians in the nineteenth did missionary work in Central America, but not among Latins. The Anglican, Lutheran, and Reformed churches, established in Latin American cities during the early part of the nineteenth century, were not evangelistic centers but rather chaplaincies for for-

eign colonies. Also, some Protestants opposed missionary work in Latin America. In the great World
Missionary Conference, held in Edinburgh in 1910,
Latin America was not even included on the agenda,
due to the objection of Lutherans and Anglicans.[1]

Furthermore, there were circumstances in Central America that made it difficult for Protestantism to
assume a missionary character: religious liberty, even
after independence, was usually limited, if existent at
all, and the prevailing Roman Catholicism was of Spanish origin, the most intransigent type known in history.
There was a general feeling that Roman Catholicism
formed an integral part of Spanish-American culture,
similar to what the Hebrew religion is for the Jews. So
there were many Latin Americans who felt that one
who converted to Protestantism was a traitor to his
race and culture.

But the picture was changing. On the one hand,
at the beginning of the nineteenth century a surge of
missionary fervor was rising among Protestants in general, growing more and more intense as the century
progressed and reaching its peak at the end of that
century and the beginning of the twentieth. On the
other hand, the rigid resistance and blind prejudice of
Latin Americans were beginning to wane. This was due
to various reasons: (1) the growth of liberalism, which
often led to anticlericalism, and (2) the "defanatization"
of the populace.

Pioneers—the Bible Societies

Another notable coincidence in the history of
Latin American Protestantism is the fact that the ori-

gin of the two principal Bible societies and the Wars for Independence were contemporary events. The British and Foreign Bible Society was born in 1804 and the American Bible Society in 1816. These societies were the first Protestant entities to show interest in the evangelization of Latin America. Soon after their origin they began to publish the Scriptures in Spanish and Portugese.

In 1823 the then recently founded American Board of Commissioners for Foreign Missions sent Theophilus Parvin and John Brigham to Spanish America to investigate the possibilities of Bible distribution. The two societies provided them with an ample supply of Scriptures. On his return in 1826, Brigham informed the tenth annual meeting of the American Society:

> We behold fifteen millions of human beings . . . professedly Christian, believing in revelation, baptized in the name of the Trinity and yet almost entirely without the Bible. . . .
>
> Throughout the long road from Buenos Aires to Chile, excepting a few in Mendoza, not a solitary book of God was found and I more than once presented copies to aged priests tottering over the grave who told me they had never seen it in their native language.[2]

In Central America the situation was no different. When the first evangelical missionaries (William and Minnie McConnell) arrived in Costa Rica in 1891, "there were no Bibles to be found anywhere among the natives," according to Mrs. McConnell's unpublished memoirs. It is no wonder, then, that the Bible societies felt that these lands were legitimate fields for their ministry.

The British Society took a special interest in South America. James Thomson, a Scottish Baptist minister, became the representative of both the Bible Society and the Lancasterian school system. He arrived first in Argentina, where he began his ministry, and then went on to Uruguay and other new republics in western South America, doing a remarkable work selling Bibles and establishing Lancasterian schools with the backing of the leaders in these republics, who were concerned about the extremely high percentage of illiteracy in their countries.[3]

The British Society also took an interest in Central America. In 1827 and 1828, during the liberal era of Morazán and Gálvez, an Englishman visited Guatemala and sold Bibles. According to his report, congress revealed interest in the establishment of Lancasterian schools and in 1832 several were established.[4]

A small Bible Society was formed in Belize when a dissolute British sailor, Frederick Crowe, was converted and became a Bible colporteur. He courageously entered Guatemala during the clerical regime of Rafael Carrera (which had replaced the original liberal administration) to sell Bibles, first in Salamá (1843) and then in the capital. Here he became professor of English and French at the University. He also began to teach music and organized the first band in the history of Guatemala, for which he had to import instruments. Furthermore, he quietly formed a group of evangelical disciples.

Crowe also asked permission to establish a Lancasterian school. He obtained permission and opened the school but soon ran into difficulties. The archbishop heard of the school and protested, alleging that

Crowe was an "Anglican priest" (when in reality he was a Baptist layman) sent from London who "has flooded the diocese with prohibited Bibles, books and pamphlets."

This protest, presented to the conservative Carrera administration, was successful. The government ordered the closing of the school (1846) and the expulsion of Crowe. And so came to an end the brief ministry of the man who is considered the precursor of the evangelical movement in Guatemala. But Crowe's influence survived. He had formed an enthusiastic group of disciples that undoubtedly was responsible in part for the liberal reform movement that in 1871 overthrew the conservative regime. Among these disciples was the brilliant statesman and writer Lorenzo Montúfar.[5]

The British Society distributed the Scriptures in Costa Rica as well, many years before the arrival of a professional evangelical missionary. Their agent was none other than the previously mentioned English sea captain, William Le Lacheur, who took Costa Rican coffee to London and brought back English merchandise and volumes of the Scriptures. Between 1846 and 1848 he sold 4,000 copies of the New Testament and 500 of the entire Bible in this little country whose population was then only 95,000.[6]

About 1854 D. H. Wheeler, chaplain to the sailors in Aspinwall, Panama, began cooperating with the American Bible Society by distributing Scriptures along the line of the trans-isthmian railroad then under construction. In 1856 he was commissioned as agent of the society for all of Central America and was sent to Nicaragua. About the same time William Walker and his "filibusters" arrived in Nicaragua at the invitation of the Liberal Party. Wheeler was in Granada, the center of the conservatives, who ordered every able-bodied man to join the forces against Walker. Wheeler refused to obey, alleging that he was an American and thus neutral. Consequently he was shot and his death brought to an end the first attempt to establish a Bible agency in Nicaragua.[7]

The most famous and beloved Bible colportur in Central America was Francisco Penzotti. Born in Italy in 1851, at the age of thirteen he emigrated to Uruguay. While still a young man, he was converted to the evangelical faith and became very active in his new faith. After a number of years as pastor in the Waldensian colony, he began working with the American Bible Society and became the boldest and most effective colporteur the society has ever known, as well as an outstanding hero in the history of the evangelical cause in Latin America.

Penzotti arrived in Central America for the first time in 1892 and established a Bible agency in Guatemala City. He was director of the Central American agency until 1917 and was a tremendous help to the early missionaries in getting the evangelical cause under way. His life was filled with thrilling as well as difficult experiences in the distribution of the Scriptures throughout these needy republics. He made himself dear to all evangelicals, so much so that he was called the "Apostle John to the Central American [Evangelical] churches."[8]

The Bible societies have continued to be one of the main factors in the development of the evangelical movement, due to the importance that evangelicals give to the Word of God. These societies have been the "right hand" of the mission societies.

At first the Church of Rome considered the work of the Bible societies to be noxious. Priests thundered against it and ordered those of the faithful who had purchased copies of the Scriptures to commit them to the flames. This was not strange, since Gregory XV had condemned the societies in his encyclical Inter Praecipuas (1844), as had Pious IX in his *Syllabus Errorum* (1869).[9] But recent years have seen a radical change of attitude, especially since Vatican Council II. The popular Spanish version of the New Testament (*Dios llega al hombre*) has received ecclesiastical approbation. Many priests now decidedly approve the efforts of the societies to distribute the Scriptures, even permitting representatives to see Bibles at the doors of their churches. Priests and monks are now among the best clients of the Bible societies.

Pioneers: Two Mission Boards

Protestant mission boards delayed in sending personnel to Latin America, especially to Central America. So great was the neglect of Central America that C. I. Scofield, when he became interested in this part of the world, exclaimed: "We have passed over our Samaria!"

The first mission board to break this indifference was that of the Northern Presbyterian Church, which in 1882 sent the first evangelical missionary to Central America for ministry to the Latin Americans. The occasion of his coming, however, was related to the political situation of that time. The clerical era in

Guatemala (1839–71) came to an end with the coup d'etat of García Granados, which inaugurated a long period of liberalism and even anticlericalism. Liberalism received a further boost with the election of Justo Rufino Barrios as president (1873). Barrios put into effect a series of drastic reforms, among which was a decree of absolute religious liberty (1873) motivated in part by his desire to facilitate Protestant immigration.[10] Naturally, the conservatives opposed the measure.

At that time a North American family named Cleaves was living on the Alameda ranch near Chimaltenango, not far from the capital. Mrs. Cleaves became an intimate friend of Mrs. Barrios. One day (about October 1881) she was at lunch in the president's home. Barrios entered the house much upset with the opposition of the clerical party to his program of reforms. Mrs. Cleaves remarked that what Guatemalans needed was to know another form of Christianity and not only Roman Catholicism. She spoke of the beneficent work of evangelical missions in Mexico and Colombia.

These words made a deep impression on the president. He asked Mrs. Cleaves to get in touch with some mission board. Being a Presbyterian, she recommended the board of her own church. Barrios wrote to Lorenzo Montúfar, his minister in Washington, asking him to contact the Presbyterian Board. A short time later the president himself was in Washington to settle a boundary dispute between Mexico and Guatemala and personally urged the board to send a missionary.

The board decided to send John Hill, previously a candidate for China. At the insistence of Barrios, Hill accompanied his party on their return to Guatemala.

So the president on his return brought with him not only a treaty with Mexico but also an evangelical missionary.[11]

Hill started his work among the Protestant foreigners in the capital, beginning public worship and a pastoral ministry among the members of the foreign colony. The president provided him with protection but this soon became unnecessary.[12] The English services resulted in the foundation of a church that functions to this day under the name of "Union Church."[13]

At the suggestion of Barrios, Hill then opened a school. This was not a strange request, since the education facilities in Guatemala were either lamentable or nonexistent. (It is estimated that in 1871, ninety-seven percent of the population was illiterate.)[14] For a nominal sum Barrios rented to Hill a two-story house that he owned. The president matriculated his own children there and suggested to the ministers of his cabinet that they do the same. The school was named *Colegio Americano*; instruction was given in English by three North American women.[15]

Later Hill attempted to start missionary work among the nationals. He wrote messages which were published in the newspaper *Diario de Centro América*, printed a few tracts, and began to hold services in Spanish, naming a Mexican evangelical as pastor and paying his entire salary. He ordained as elder the janitor of the school. As it was mostly the poor who attended the meetings, Hill, undoubtedly well intentioned, began to help them economically. The result was the rise of a group of so-called "rice Christians." When economic help was not forthcoming, their interest in the gospel waned correspondingly, especially with the rise of persecution.

While Hill's social contacts were people of high society, his missionary work was among the poor. When the mission board did not send all the money he requested, financial difficulties developed. Further, in 1885 Barrios, Hill's sponsor and protector, was killed in a war for the union of all of Central America. Apparently, because of Hill's lack of success as a missionary and his financial embarrassment, he left Guatemala and returned to the United States.

The Presbyterian Board did not become discouraged with Guatemala as a mission field, even though its first experience had been disappointing. To the contrary, they sent Edward Haymaker, a missionary of some experience in Mexico, to take Hill's place. (The Presbyterians had been in Mexico since 1872.) Haymaker arrived in 1887 and began his ministry more wisely. He converted the *Colegio* into a school for poor children, and revived the ill-founded congregation of Spanish-speaking people. He obtained property near the center of town that had been a monastery but had been confiscated by the government, and built a chapel there. In 1889 he launched an evangelical periodical, *El Mensajero*, and started a vocational school. Soon he was making evangelistic trips into different parts of the country. At the invitation of the liberals, he founded a church in Quetzaltenango, which became an important center of the Presbyterian Mission. Little by little Haymaker established a solid and robust evangelical work.[16]

The second evangelical organization to start work in Central America was the Central American

Mission. This mission was not founded by a denomination but rather by Cyrus I. Scofield, pastor of the First Congregational Church of Dallas, Texas, who later edited the well-known Scofield Reference Bible and became the principal exponent of the dispensationalist interpretation of the Bible. Scofield himself had been greatly influenced while attending missionary conferences, especially through the messages of Hudson Taylor.[17]

Scofield was impressed by the fact that, even though Central America was a near neighbor, there was little or no evangelical missionary activity in this area. He determined to organize a mission for this purpose and chose Costa Rica as the place to begin its ministry.[18]

The first missionary was William McConnell, a Presbyterian layman from St. Paul, Minnesota. He had been active in Christian service, especially in the Y.M.C.A.; however, he had no formal theological training but was self-taught and apparently a follower of Scofield's interpretation of the Bible.[19]

Dispensationalism spurred missionary zeal but also sometimes resulted in superficial work and a neglect of missionary and ecclesiastical aspects not related directly to evangelism. This was caused largely by its emphasis on the imminence of the return of Christ. This is precisely what happened in the beginning of the work of the Central American Mission.

McConnell arrived in Costa Rica on February 24, 1891. Other missionaries soon followed, so that by 1895 there were nine in the country.[20] Zealous in their evangelism, by the end of the century they had covered much of the country, spreading tracts, holding evangelistic meetings, and doing personal witnessing. By 1900 they had baptized 190 "believers," organized four churches, and formed a notable group of national evangelists and leaders.[21]

Not until 1896 did the mission enter another republic, when, in July, four missionaries came to Santa Rosa de Copán, Honduras: Albert E. Bishop, his wife, Belle Purves, and Dora Shipp. By the end of the century there were eleven missionaries in the country. They lived in extremely difficult circumstances and were plagued with tropical diseases, causing the death of two of them.[22] But as a result of their work they had 295 "baptized believers."[23]

The ministry of the Central American Mission in El Salvador was also begun in the midst of tragedy. The first couple destined for El Salvador was H. C. Dillon and his wife. In 1894, while sailing for the Pacific port of Acajutla, Mrs. Dillon died and was buried at sea.[24] Dillon returned temporarily to the United States.

In 1896 Samuel Purdie, a veteran missionary of the Friends (Quakers) who had been serving in Mexico for twenty-four years, came to El Salvador.[25] He found an open door and visited many villages. After some time in the country he wrote that "up to the present I have not found one person who has read the Bible." He set up a printing press and among the books he published was a hymnal. One day, while setting type, he cut his finger. A few days later lockjaw developed, resulting in his death, barely a year after beginning a promising ministry in that little republic.[26]

In 1897 Robert Bender began a missionary career in El Salvador that lasted fifty years and won for him the title of "the beloved apostle of El Salvador."[27] Yet in 1900 after four years of labor, there were only thirty-two baptized believers in the republic.[28]

In 1896 H. C. Dillon returned to Central America with his new wife. At first they settled in Guatemala, but after six months they moved to Honduras where Dillon later died.[29]

Thus, it was not until 1899 that the Central American Mission began a permanent work in Guatemala, when Albert Bishop, after three years in Honduras, moved to the neighboring republic. Within six months he already had a preaching center in the capital at *Cinco Calles*, a place near the center of town where "five streets" converged. At first there was violent opposition until the authorities intervened and the violence subsided. Within a few weeks twenty people had made profession of faith. The preaching continued for 150 consecutive nights.[30]

Guatemala proved to be more receptive to the gospel than any of the other republics. J. G. Cassel, who came to Guatemala shortly after Bishop, wrote in 1905 that three years previously, on traveling the 135 miles from Guatemala City to San Marcos, one met very few believers; but "now there is almost a continuous chain of towns where one is welcomed by believers and where already exist the nuclei of what are to be hoped will become flourishing churches of the future."[31]

Nicaragua was the last of the five republics entered by the Central American Mission. In 1900 A. B. Roos and his wife were sent to Nicaragua where they encountered heavy opposition. Nevertheless by the middle of 1901 there were fifteen candidates for baptism and others interested.[32]

The Plymouth Brethren also entered Central America before the end of the century. By the year 1898 they had established a work in San Pedro Sula, which, however, enjoyed little success.[33] In 1896 William Arthur, a "brother" from Philadelphia, Pennsylvania, attempted to found an "industrial mission" in the northern part of Costa Rica as a means of helping the Guatuso Indians who were living in misery. From Greytown, accompanied by a number of neophyte helpers, he went up the San Juan River, then southward up the *Río Frío* into northern Costa Rica. Unfortunately, the well-intentioned project died aborning: the northern whites were unable to endure the hot, humid climate of the jungle and the primitive mode of life.[34]

The Seventh-day Adventists began to spread their message in Central America before the end of the century as well, first of all among the West Indians along the Caribbean Coast. In 1891 they already had missions on the Bay Islands of Honduras and in 1897 had a boat ministry that made stops along the coast as far south as Colón, Panama.[35]

Thus, it is evident that at the end of the nineteenth century Protestantism was attempting to bring its message to the Latin Americans themselves in Central America through the efforts of one denomination (two if we include the Seventh-day Adventists) and two independent missions. The beginnings, however, were weak. The missionaries encountered strong opposition from both the laity and clergy of the Roman Catholic Church. They also suffered from the weather, which was inclement for northerners. Consequently the results of their work were exiguous.

IV

Advance in the Midst of Opposition

At the beginning of the twentieth century the evangelical cause began to advance with vigor in Guatemala but more slowly in the other Central American Republics. In Guatemala the evangelical movement experienced extraordinary progress during the first thirty-five years of the century. The two pioneer missions realized a wide and effective work. At the end of 1935 the Central American Mission had 63 organized churches and 185 preaching centers with a total of 13,700 members and ahherents. It had also begun to show a slight social dimension, establishing schools in Guatemala City (1915), San Antonio de Aguas Claras (1919), and Huehuetenango (1920). It likewise had set up medical dispensaries in the last two mentioned places, and in 1929 founded a Bible Institute in the capital for the preparation of national pastors.[1]

The Presbyterians also prospered. By the end of 1935 they had 22 organized churches and 198 preaching centers with 10,082 members and adherents.[2] The first presbytery was organized in 1923 and a second in 1927.[3] They also established a number of prestigious schools and a hospital of high caliber in the capital (1913).[4]

Both missions revealed concern for the native Indians who composed approximately 60 percent of the population of the country. In 1923 the Central American Mission started a Bible Institute in Panajachel for the Indians. Cameron Townsend, of the same mission (who later founded the renowned "Summer Institute of Linguistics"), translated the New Testament into the language of the Cakchikels, which was published in 1931. Some time later the New Testament was translated into Quiché by Mrs. Paul Burgess and into Mam by Horace Peck, both of the Presbyterian Mission.[5]

Other groups began to show interest in Central America. In 1901 John Butler and his wife came to Guatemala from a Pentecostal Mission in Nashville, Tennessee, and settled in an area northwest of Guatemala City. In 1915 this mission was taken over by the Church of the Nazarene and extended northward to Alta y Baja Verapaz and Petén, with the city of Cobán as center. The Nazarenes also enjoyed success with the result that in 1936 they had twenty-one churches and seventy preaching points with 3,250 members and adherents.[6]

In 1901 A. E. Bishop of the Central American Mission spoke about the evangelical cause in Guatemala at the Friends' Training School for Christian workers located in Whittier, California. Two students, Thomas Kelly and Clark Buckley, were so deeply impressed that the following year they headed for Chiquimula (a town located about seventy-five kilometers southeast of the capital) with a ton of Bibles and started the mission of their denomination in Guatemala. Sad to say, at the end of two years their efforts had come to an end, due perhaps to the naiveté of the students. Later the work was renewed, when formal missionaries were sent. Among them was an outstanding woman, Ruth Esther Smith, who became a kind of matriarch for the Friends in Guatemala.[7]

The Friends were fervent evangelists. In 1921 they had 1,858 members in their churches. By 1936 this number had increased to 8,400 members and adherents.[8] The Friends also emphasized education, establishing schools for both girls and boys. In 1921 they founded a *Colegio Bíblico* in Chiquimula for the preparation of national pastors, the first institution of this kind in central America.[9]

By 1911 the work of the Friends had spread into Honduras where it enjoyed some success. By 1936 there were 2,500 members and adherents in their community.[10] About 1915 the Friends entered El Salvador, but here the progress was meager: by 1936 they had only 350 adherents.[11]

In 1916 Charles T. Furnam came to Guatemala under the auspices of a Pentecostal group in the USA. Unable to continue their mission, the Pentecostals turned it over to the Free Methodists in 1921, but Furnam continued with the Methodists. Their ministry was principally among the Quiché Indians. Eventually doctrinal differences arose between the Pentecostal Furnam and the Methodists. In 1932 the churches under Furnam's supervision experienced an "outpour-

ing in tongues. The Free Methodists were displeased
with this phenomenon and consequently discharged
missionary Furnam, who with a number of churches
decided to affiliate with the Church of God (Cleveland,
Tenn.). Thus, the Church of God began its work in
Guatemala in 1935.[12]

It is noteworthy that these three groups (Nazarenes, Friends, and Free Methodists) adhered to Armi-
nian theology with its emphasis on the free will of man
and the consequent doctrine that one can "fall from
grace." They also sustained the ultra-Wesleyan doctrine
of "entire sanctification" as a postconversion experience. To the contrary, the Presbyterians and the Central
American Mission were Calvinists and rejected both
doctrines. Nevertheless, these doctrinal differences did
not hinder the later union of the five groups into an
"Evangelical Synod" in 1935 (see next chapter).

We have already made passing reference to the
Pentecostals. This sector of Protestantism is distin-
guished by its emphasis on "divine healing" and the
doctrine of the "baptism of the Holy Spirit" as an experience subsequent to justification (conversion). The
Pentecostal movement, as we know it today, began in
California about 1906. A few years later, and during the
period now under consideration, there were sporadic
manifestations of Pentecostalism in Central America,
perhaps in every republic. But during the final period
of our study it became a major force (numerically), as
we shall see.

The strongest Pentecostal denomination is the
Assemblies of God, which began its labors in El Salva-
dor. About 1912 an independent Canadian missionary,
Federico Medios, came to this republic. He had re-

cently experienced the "baptism of the Holy Spirit." Through his preaching hundreds were converted. But his fervor and the noisy character of their meetings were offensive to the public; consequently, they suffered persecution, at times instigated by the priests.

For many years the Pentecostals were disorganized, drifting along until 1929, when they united with the Mission Board of the Assemblies of God. Under the wise direction of the first missionary, Ralf Williams, the Pentecostals received the orientation they needed.[13] Under good organization, as well as enthusiasm, the work prospered. By 1936 the Assemblies had 965 members and adherents in 21 churches.[14]

The Assemblies also began a work in Nicaragua, but it met with little success. In 1936 it had only fifty members and adherents in one church and two preaching centers.[15]

Many of the West Indians who came to Central America at the end of the nineteenth century were Baptists, and among the first colporteurs and missionaries there were also a few Baptists. However, it was not until 1911 that the Baptists formally began missionary efforts among the Spanish-speaking Central Americans.

In El Salvador some independent evangelicals expressed a desire to form part of a real denomination, "preferably Baptist." One of their representatives, Emilio Morales, informed the Mission Board of the Northern Baptist Convention in the USA of this desire. The board replied quickly and named as its missionary a British Baptist, William Keech, at that time a representative of the British Bible Society in the republic.[16] At first Keech was alone except for the help of a fellow countryman, a pensioned British soldier residing in the country. But soon North American missionaries arrived.[17]

According to an official report by the Mission Board, "the work prospered from the very beginning. Small groups of believers, lost in the mountains and valleys, invited the missionaries to visit them and explain more clearly the Scriptures."[18] By 1936 there were 2,200 members and adherents in the Baptist churches of El Salvador which were now an organized convention.[19] The Baptists emphasized education and established a number of prestigious schools.

In 1916 the "Congress on Christian Work in Latin America," an evangelical ecumenical conference, was held in Panama. One result of the congress was an attempt to make a "comity" distribution of Central American countries among the mission boards of Protestant denominations. El Salvador, Honduras, and Nicaragua were assigned to the Northern Baptists.[20]

Previous to this comity arrangement there had been some Baptist activity in Nicaragua among the English-speaking inhabitants on Corn Island. Now with the official assignment, the Baptist Mission Board began to send missionaries to Nicaragua and soon the Baptists were established in Managua, Masaya, Diriamba, and León.[21]

The missionaries met resistance, sometimes violent, from the Church of Rome. Furthermore, internal problems arose: in 1918 a national pastor withdrew to form a schismatic group called "The Independent Baptist Evangelical Church."[22] Nevertheless, the work prospered. A group of capable national pastors arose, among whom stood out Arturo Parajón. By 1936 there were

1,810 members and adherents in eight churches and preaching points.[23] In 1937 these churches also organized a convention.[24]

Nicaraguan Baptists from the beginning revealed a social dimension. The *Colegio Bautista* had a humble origin in 1916,[25] but became one of the best high schools in the republic. In 1930 a Baptist hospital was inaugurated, another institution that brought honor to the Baptist cause.[26]

According to the disposition of the Panama Congress, Honduras was assigned to the Northern Baptists but they never did occupy this territory.[27] The first denominational mission to enter Honduras was the Evangelical Synod—a denomination composed of German immigrants to the USA, basically Lutheran but influenced by Calvinism. The Synod came to Honduras at the request of a Honduranian, Ramón Guzmán, who had been converted through the ministry of Fred Lincoln of the Central American Mission. Guzmán became an ardent advocate of his new faith. During a trip to Washington, D.C., about 1919, he met by coincidence the Executive Secretary of the Mission Board of the Evangelical Synod. Guzmán presented to him the need of the gospel in Northern Honduras and urged the board to send missionaries to that part of his country. His challenge was accepted and in 1921 the first missionaries, Harold Auler and family, and Anna Bechthold, arrived. In March of that year they settled in San Pedro Sula, the city that became the center of the mission.[28]

Immediately, even before beginning public meetings, they opened a school that in the course of time became one of the most outstanding educational institutions in the country. Education came to be one of the principal emphases of the mission.[29]

In May of 1921 they held the initial public service. The first converts were baptized in November of 1925, and in August of the following year the first church of the Synod in Honduras was organized with twenty-six members.[30] But the church work progressed slowly. In 1936, fifteen years after the coming of the pioneer missionaries, there were only 250 communicants and adherents in three churches and five preaching centers.[31]

In 1934 the mother church in the USA joined with the Reformed Church (a denomination of German Calvinists) to form the Evangelical and Reformed Church, a name the Honduranian group retains to this day, even though in 1957 the mother church joined with the Congregational Christian Church to form the United Church of Christ.

The Panamanian Congress of 1916, in its distribution of Central America, assigned to the Methodist Episcopal Church (today the United Methodist Church) Panama and Costa Rica. Since 1906 this denomination had sustained a small mission in Panama that consisted of a church established to minister to the many who had come for the construction of the Panama Canal.[32] The decision of the Congress gave incentive to the Methodists to extend their work in Panama and to enter Costa Rica. In 1917 George Miller, superintendent in Panama, together with Eduardo Zapata, an outstanding Methodist leader in Mexico, visited Costa Rica. They began immediately to hold public services. In 1919 they purchased the edifice of the Club Centro Catalán, located on Central Avenue toward the east, and remodeled it for church services.

Soon thereafter they purchased properties in Alajuela, San Ramón, and Barrio México (a suburb of San José). In spite of much economic help the Methodist mission progressed very slowly. In 1933, after sixteen years of labor, there were only 125 communicants in the Methodist Episcopal Church of Costa Rica, with an average attendance of 273 in their Sunday Schools.[33] In Panama the picture was not much better. After thirty years there were only 378 communicant members.[34]

The Methodists, according to their tradition, immediately showed concern for the social welfare of the people to whom they had come. This was evident in their propaganda in favor of temperance, the establishment of schools both in Costa Rica (1921) and Panama, and the promotion of the Boy Scout movement in Costa Rica (1923).[35]

In 1921 a new and extraordinarily energetic type of mission was established in Costa Rica, one that would influence greatly the evangelical cause, not only in Central America, but in all of Spanish America: the Latin America Evangelistic Campaign (a name that was later changed to the Latin America Mission). The founders, Harry (Scottish) and Susan (Irish) Strachan, had already served for some sixteen years with the Regions Beyond Mission (a British organization) in Argentina. They were greatly perturbed by the slowness of the evangelization of Latin America. (It seemed as if many evangelicals, after suffering so much scorn, prejudice, and persecution, were possessed by a kind of inferiority complex.) The Strachans were convinced that what was lacking was a more aggressive type of evangelism. So they separated peacefully from their mission to dedicate themselves precisely to this need.[36]

They decided to promote evangelistic campaigns on a large scale, employing leading Spanish-American preachers and using any and every legitimate means of publicity to attract the populace. Strachan recruited as evangelists such eloquent orators as Juan Varetto, a Baptist from Argentina, Angel Archilla Cabrera, a Presbyterian from Puerto Rico, Roberto Elfick Valenzuela, a Methodist from Chile, and Samuel Palomeque from Spain. They preached in theaters, tents, and in the open air. Popular music, fireworks, handbills, and so forth were used to attract crowds.

During the years 1921–34 Strachan directed a series of remarkable campaigns in fourteen of the twenty Spanish-American republics. Never before had there been such a large and bold evangelistic endeavor. Hundreds of people professed the evangelical faith and thousands heard the gospel for the first time.[37] In my opinion, these campaigns gave a tremendous boost to the evangelical movement and were one of the factors in its modern phenomenal advance, which began approximately in 1935.

The headquarters of the campaign were in San José, Costa Rica. Here, under the guidance of Mrs. Strachan, began a number of institutions that would contribute greatly to the progress of the evangelical cause both inside and outside of Costa Rica. In 1923 a little Bible School was started under her direction that eventually developed into the well-known *Seminario Bíblico Latinoamericano*, an institution that produced many leaders for the evangelical movement in Latin

America. In 1929 the *Clínica Bíblica* was inaugurated, a hospital tht helped elevate the standards of medical attention in Costa Rica. The same year the *Templo Bíblico* was constructed, the largest Protestant chapel in all of Central America at that time. This big building became necessary because of the many converts during the campaign that was held in San José in 1927.[38] And in 1932 the "campaign" established an orphanage (*Hogar Bíblico*) on the side of Mount Barba, approximately twelve miles northwest of San José.[39]

Reference should also be made to the Seventh-day Adventists, who before had worked only among the English-speaking people. During this period they extended their activities to the Spanish-speaking Central Americans.[40] In 1906 the Adventists of the Caribbean had organized the West Indian Union Conference by joining the five Adventist conferences and four mission fields in this area. The headquarters were first established in Kingston, Jamaica, but in 1908 they were transferred to Colón, Panama.[41] With this step Adventist missionary activities were accelerated in Central America. By 1936 they had churches in Guatemala with 600 members and adherents, in El Salvador with 545, in Honduras with 250, in Nicaragua with 275, in Costa Rica with 350, and in Panama with 5,119.[42] It should be remembered that a high percentage of the Adventists in Central America at that time were of West Indian origin.

The Adventists were outstanding in stewardship (tithing was obligatory for a genuine church member) and in their social work, especially regarding their emphasis on physical health.

With the center of their "Union" in Panama,

Costa Rica became a next-door neighbor. The decision was made to set up a vocational school in said republic, which was established first in San José in 1927, moved later to San Ramón de Tres Ríos, and finally to Alajuela in 1950.[43] In Puerto Cabezas, Nicaragua, the Adventists built a hospital, although they later sold it to the Moravians (1956).[44]

V

Characteristics of the Early Evangelicals[1]

Of Humble Origin

Most of those who accepted the evangelical faith were of lowly origin. There were reasons for this. The Roman Catholic religion and the Spanish-American race and culture were so intimately related that members of the upper classes were fearful of identifying themselves with evangelicals for social reasons. The poor man had much less to lose in this matter. Furthermore, he had been neglected by the Church of Rome due to the scarcity of priests or lack of sacerdotal interest. The poor, therefore, were a fertile field for the missionaries. Even so, many of the humble folk were also fearful of the stigma that resulted in associating with evangelicals.

Another reason for the gospel's appeal to the poor was that in the membership of an evangelical church, which usually was small, the poor person was of some importance and was not lost in the anonymity of a large Catholic church. He was taken into account and given something to do. He sang choruses and hymns in the services, gave his testimony, was asked to pray, and sometimes was given material help, although the latter was to become a source of difficulties for the evangelical missionary. While some natives were afraid to associate with the evangelicals for fear of disdain or persecution, others pretended interest in the gospel for the material help that this might gain for them. There were "rice Christians" in Central America also. When the help ceased, the "interest" in the gospel also ceased.

Liberals and anticlericals favored and defended the evangelicals; not necessarily because of sympathy with evangelical doctrine but rather because of their belief in religious liberty and their common enmity toward clericalism, as in the case of Justo Rufino Barrios (see pp. 30ff.). The few that sympathized with the gospel message also feared the stigma of being linked with evangelicals.

Polemics

The first missionaries, pastors, and lay people in Central America were characterized by a marked polemical spirit. They were violently opposed to the theology and practice of the Church of Rome. Precisely because they considered Roman Catholicism fraught with error they believed that the evangelical movement was necessary. Besides the historic differences between Protestantism and Romanism (bibliological, soteriological, and ecclesiological), in Central America there were features of Spanish-American Catholicism that the evangelicals attacked virulently: the mariological excesses ("mariolatry," according to the evangelicals), the veneration of saints, images, and relics ("idolatry" for the evangelicals), syncretism with Indian worship (especially in Guatemala), and the pompous and external character of Spanish-American worship (e.g., the frequent processions). The evangelicals charged that these characteristics did away with the centrality of Christ and were not in accord with the essentially spiritual character of Christian worship.

Further, they pointed out the ignorance that existed concerning the regenerating and sanctifying work of the Holy Spirit and the new life in Christ. They called attention to the lack of the use of the Bible in public worship and to the general illiteracy of the faithful concerning its contents. They also criticized the low morals of both the clergy and the laity. (It should be pointed out that this criticism came not only from the evangelicals but also from liberals and Catholics in other parts of the world.) The evangelicals also remonstrated against the rift that existed between morals and religion. (A patent example of this was the distinction often made between the priest behind the altar and the priest in the street.) They affirmed that religiosity and sanctimoniousness were not accompanied by true Christian conduct and morals.

Evangelistic Zeal

If on the one hand some were timid and fearful in revealing their new faith, on the other hand there were those who were enthusiastic, bold, and sometimes imprudent in their desire to propagate the gospel. They were constantly doing personal evangelism, giving out tracts and Scripture portions, preaching on the streets when permitted, or holding services in private homes. If these were rented, the owners sometimes objected and threatened to evict the renters if they continued the practice.

Pietism and Puritanism

Many of the first groups and denominations concerned about the evangelization of Spanish America were pietists or puritans in their moral standards and emphasized a radical conversion and rigorous morals. The converts to the evangelical faith were required to make a complete break with the "world" as well as with their old religious system. Here we most likely have another reason why church membership increased so slowly. The requisites for baptism were so high that many were afraid to become candidates for church membership; consequently, there were many "unbaptized believers."

Marital fidelity was also required, as was abstinence from alcoholic drinks and tobacco, and immodest dress. Some things that were prohibited by evangelicals were permitted or considered *adiaphora* by Catholics (and some Protestant churches)—such as dancing, theater going, and the use of cosmetics. (We are speaking of the primitive evangelicals. In recent years extreme puritanism has been disappearing.)

On the one hand, it is true that this puritanism

sometimes produced hypocrisy and resulted in "straining out the gnat and swallowing the camel." On the other hand, it also explained why many evangelicals were able to rise out of their poverty. Instead of wasting his meager salary in vices, which in turn were hurtful to his health, the believer, following the "Protestant ethic," was now able to do better by his family, earn more, save more, and as a result prosper economically and rise culturally.

Emphasis on Justification by Faith

Central American evangelicalism, in consonance with the keynote of the Protestant Reformation, emphasized the fact that salvation is not the result of a cooperative effort on the part of God and man, transmitted by the sacramental intervention of priests, but is rather a free gift that a person receives on repentance and faith in Jesus Christ. It also taught that it is possible to enjoy the assurance of salvation. At the same time it taught that conversion produes a change in one's manner of life, resulting in good works. But it insisted that these are the result and not a cause of salvation.

Roman Catholic Reaction

At the beginning the clergy unanimously was alarmed at the "invasion" of evangelical missionaries in territory that for centuries had been the exclusive domain of Roman and Hispanic Catholicism. Pluralism was something unthinkable for them.

Their first accusation was, of course, that Protestant teaching was heretical. To the priests of that time the worst thing had happened to Central America: it had been infiltrated by disciples of such heretics as Luther, Calvin, and Henry VIII. They accused the evangelicals of not believing in the Virgin, of distributing a mutilated and unauthorized Bible, of preaching the doctrine of justification by faith alone, which inevitably would produce immorality, and of denying the authority of the Pope, which automatically put them outside the pale of the true church. They also pointed out the divided condition of Protestantism as a proof of its falseness.

Another accusation was that the rise of the evangelical movement was politically and socially injurious for Central America since it threatened to destroy the unity of these countries. Some alleged that Protestant missionaries were the vanguard of foreign domination. At the end of the nineteenth century they were saying that evangelicals were preparing the way for the British dominion of Latin America. Then at the beginning of the twentieth they changed and said that they were the precursors of North American ("Yankee") imperialism. Later, with the rise of Communism, appeared the slogan that conversion to Protestantism was the first step to Communism.

Opposition to evangelicals was generally, but not always, nonviolent. One of the most common violent methods was the interruption of the services. Sometimes it was done by individuals who would throw stones on the roof of the meeting places. On occasions a zealous priest would organize a group of the faithful, force their entrance into the building where the believers were gathered and break up the meeting. There were cases in which they burned the chapel or the pastoral home, and yet others in which the evangelist was beaten up and left gravely wounded. In such cases the civil authorities usually defended the evangelicals.

The religious stigma evangelicals bore produced social problems. Their children at times suffered prejudice and even persecution in public schools. This problem motivated the construction of evangelical schools.

One of the most traumatic experiences of the early believer was that suffered by those being treated in public hospitals, which were usually managed by nuns. LeRoy McConnell, missionary in Costa Rica, in 1923 described the problem in the following manner:

> When a patient enters, one of the first things [the nuns] do is to see to it that he confesses to a priest, and if he refuses, the persecution begins. Moreover they insist on prayers before the images or in the chapel at fixed hours. As a result the evangelical Christians are mortally afraid of going there, even imagining that they might poison them to get rid of them.[2]

Such conditions motivated the establishment of more than one evangelical hospital in Central America.

Naturally, the development of the evangelical movement in such circumstances affected its character and mentality. It tended to produce a martyr complex and ghetto mentality. It became difficult for the evangelicals to enter fully in the social and political life of the country, which was so intimately related to the popular religion. The "pilgrim" character of the Christian life was profoundly felt among the early believers.

Summary of the Period

The first fifty-three years (1882–1935) of the evangelical movement in Central America were extremely difficult. Consequently its progress was meager. According to the reports of the first Latin American ecumenical evangelical congress, held in Panama in 1916, there were only 10,442 communicant members in the Protestant churches in Central America.[3] (To calculate the "Protestant Community" it is customary to multiply the number of communicant members by three.) The results of thirty-four years of labor were meager, indeed, especially when one takes into account that a large proportion of this number was made up of non-Latin Protestant immigrants and their descendants.

However, toward the end of this period the picture was improving. In spite of continued opposition, during the twenty years following the congress the evangelical movement grew appreciably. By 1936 the communicant membership of Protestants had increased to 41,188,[4] and the majority of these were Hispanics. This figure represented a "community" of approximately 125,000, or slightly under 2 percent of the population of Central America. Yet one must remember that this figure included Panama, in which 6 percent of the population was Protestant due to the presence of many foreigners.[5]

VI

Growth and Development in the Modern Period

At the end of the second period and after years of slow growth, the evangelical movement began to show signs of progress. During the third period the progress was phenomenal. According to studies made by a trio of investigators of the "Church Growth" movement[1] the number of Protestant communicants in Central America increased from 41,118 in 1936 to 187,872 in 1966, which implied a community of some 563,350. This meant that Protestants had come to constitute a little more than 4 percent of the population of Central America.

Reasons for Growth

One factor here might be the decrease in popular opposition to Protestantism. However, with this decrease was a corresponding increase in clerical opposition from 1940 to 1950, years in which the tradition anticlericalism of Central America was losing its vigor. In this new atmosphere the clergy wished to recover the terrain lost during the years of anticlericalism at the end of the nineteenth and beginning of the twentieth centuries. This growing clerical opposition experienced a notable change at the beginning of the 1960s, though, during the years of John XXIII and Vatican Council II (we shall comment on this later on).

A second factor stimulating modern growth was the aggressive evangelism spearheaded by the campaigns of Harry Strachan during the years 1921–34 (see pp. 45ff.). Twenty-five years later Harry's son Kenneth developed "Evangelism in Depth," a new method of reaching people, which also made a strong impact. The campaigns had an ecumenical character, uniting all evangelicals in a unique evangelistic effort.

Third, Central America had ceased to be a "Samaria passed over." To the contrary, an exaggerated number of Protestant missions began sending personnel to these republics. From 1936 to 1970 at least fifty additional mission boards established missions in Central America, all of them from North America;[2] this does not include the organizations coming from other parts of the world.

During the decades of 1930 and 1940 the world began to rediscover Latin America, especially the USA where this interest produced the so-called "Good Neighbor Policy." Among those who made the rediscovery were the Protestant mission boards. So great became the interest in Latin America that in 1959, 25 percent of the personnel of all Protestant mission boards was found in this part of the world; by 1969 this proportion had increased to 32 percent.[3]

It should be pointed out that this same interest had awakened not only among Protestants but also (and even more so) among North American Catholics. In 1962, the Catholic mission boards had 28 percent of their personnel in Latin America and ten years later this percentage had increased to 45. In the last mentioned year there were 728 USA Catholic missionaries in Central America.[4]

Another influential circumstance was the fact that World War II had caused the exodus of hundreds of missionaries from the Orient. A number of mission boards, in view of the new interest in Latin America, sent some of these missionaries to the lands south of the Río Grande.

Many of the new organizations were independent or "faith" missions, that is, without any direct denominational relationship. Those denominations recently showing the greatest interest in Latin America have been the Baptists and Pentecostals. Since 1936 at least ten different Baptist missions and an incalculable number of Pentecostal organizations have begun work in Central America. The evangelical wing that has extended itself the farthest is the Pentecostal movement, which constitutes the fourth factor responsible for modern expansion. In 1936 there were only 950 Pentecostal communicants in Central America, 2.3 percent of the toal number of church members.[5] But in 1965 there were 67,747, or 37 percent of the membership,[6] and the percentage is increasing. Evidently the Pentecostal customs and interpretation of the gospel were popular in Central America as well as in the rest of Latin America.

Division and Ecumenism

The evangelical forces were divided to a point of exaggeration due largely to the fact that the work had been realized almost entirely by North American Protestantism, the most pluralistic type in all the world. And in addition to the divisions brought from the USA, others were born in Central America itself.

The situation appeared to be desperate and even ridiculous. In Costa Rica, for example, a country of about 2,000,000 inhabitants and a Protestant community of approximately 80,000 in 1974, there were at least fifty Protestant groups. Of these, eight were Baptist and seventeen Pentecostal.[7]

The picture was not as dark as it might appear, however. Each group did not conceive of itself as the *una sancta*, outside of which there was no salvation (although the theology of a few approached this manner of thinking). The vast majority felt that they had a basic unity (in the midst of diversity), which was revealed in the common name by which almost all of them identified themselves: *"evangélicos"* (not *"protestantes,"* a term that had little significance for them). Nevertheless, individualism prevailed. Most groups wanted to "do their own thing." Not many were willing to sacrifice themselves for the common good.

However, large common tasks sometimes united them. During the Evangelism in Depth campaigns in Nicaragua (1960), Costa Rica (1961), Guatemala (1962), and Honduras (1964), the cooperation of the evangelicals was almost total.

But ecumenism on an ecclesiastical level has had little lasting success. The first attempt was made in

Guatemala in 1935, when the two largest groups (the Presbyterians and the Central American Mission) took steps toward the formation of a "Synod of the Evangelical Church of Guatemala," which was consummated in 1937. A short time later the Nazarenes, the Friends, and the Primitive Methodists joined the synod.[8]

In May of 1941 a notable ecumenical event was sponsored by the synod: a "Central America Evangelical Congress," which took place in the well-known *Iglesia de Cinco Calles* in Guatemala City.[9] In attendance were representatives of all the countries of Central America. The principal speaker was John R. Mott, the renowned missionary statesman, sometimes called the "father of the modern ecumenical movement" that culminated in the formation of the World Council of Churches in 1948.

However, this congress did not produce any organization for the promotion of unity in Central America. The synod itself began losing its original character. Some members feared that it would be hurtful to their own particular groups. There also arose doctrinal differences. In addition, denominations traditionally opposed to ecumenism, sucn as the Southern Baptists and Missouri Lutherans, came to Guatemala at this time. So the synod was transformed into an "Evangelical Alliance," which affected less the autonomy of each group.[10] Similar alliances appeared in Honduras, Costa Rica, and El Salvador.[11]

The most notable turn of affairs in the field of ecumenism in recent years has been the relaxation of tension between evangelicals and Catholics and the beginning of dialogue and better relations.

This change began rather suddenly. During the

first years of the present period (1935–60) it seemed
that tension was increasing. On the one hand, the
evangelical movement was growing rapidly; on the
other hand, old political and cultural liberalism was
waning and the clergy was desirous of restoring the
position that it once had in public life. In 1942 Costa
Rica, for example, abrogated some of the anticlerical
laws of 1884, in particular the prohibition of religious
instruction in public schools and the establishment of
monastic orders. As a result the clergy became more
active in the civic affairs of the nation. Then in 1953,
in an imposing ceremony, the country was dedicated
to the "Sacred Heart of Jesus," with President Otilio
Ulate, an old-time liberal, on his knees reading the
proclamation.[12]

In Honduras, a country whose religious condition
had been deplorable, a similar ceremony took place in
the midst of a religious revival in 1959. President Vil-
leda Morales (also known as a liberal) joined with Archbishop Morales in the dedication of the nation to the
Immaculate Heart of Mary as well as to the Sacred
Heart of Jesus.[13]

Naturally, this revival of the ancient type of
Roman Catholicism affected the evangelical movement. Old tensions revived. In Costa Rica persecution
motivated the foundation of a new evangelical school
(1955) where the children of believers could study un-
molested, without having to obtain special permission
to absent themselves from religious instruction
classes.[14]

However, in the early 1960s these tensions began
to decrease. The principal factor in this change was the

new Pope, John XXIII, and Vatican Council II, whose effects were soon felt in Central America.

One of the first symptoms of this change in Costa Rica was José Míguez Bonino's visit to the Roman Catholic Seminary in San José on May 25, 1963. Dr. Míguez, rector of the Evangelical faculty of theology in Buenos Aries, had been the only Protestant observer from Latin America at Vatican Council II. On his return from Rome he visited San José. The rector of the Catholic Seminary, Dr. José Pauels, an ecumenically minded German, learned of Míguez' visit and invited him to give a report on the council to the faculty and students of the seminary. Míguez arrived accompanied by professors from the Biblical Seminary (LAM) of San José and the Methodist Seminary of Alajuela.[15] This dramatic encounter initiated a period of friendly relations between these institutions. Subsequently, incident after incident revealed that a new day was dawning in regard to relations between Catholics and Protestants.

Before the Vatican Council a Bible study movement had already begun in the Church of Rome but afterward it grew phenomenally. Previously the clergy had violently attacked the work of the Bible societies; now they were among their best clients.

The Costa Rican weekly, *Eco Católico*, stopped attacking the evangelicals and began to make favorable comments about them. On October 29, 1967, Dr. Pauels attended the cornerstone-laying service for the new Lutheran church in Curridabat. In this service the congregation sang "A Mighty Fortress is our God," the battle-cry hymn of the Reformation. In 1968 there were ecumenical worship services both in the Metropolitan

Cathedral and the Episcopal Church. From 1963 on for a number of years Presidential Breakfasts brought Catholics and Protestants together.

Among university students an interconfessional group called *"Agape"* was formed. Speakers at the inauguration of the *Agape* "Coffee House" were Rubén Lores, rector of the *Seminario Bíblico* and Carlos J. Alfaro, the parish priest of San Pedro de Montes de Oca.

Some Protestants and Catholics found common ground in the Charismatic Movement. A Dominican monk, Francis McNutt, started the movement in Costa Rica while on a visit in 1971. During his visit he preached in the Templo Bíblico—the first time a Catholic priest had filled the pulpit of this church, where for many years the Church of Rome had been castigated frequently and violently.

Ecclesiastical, Institutional, and Social Progress

Since 1936 evangelical churches have progressed in every aspect of their life, developing numerous and varied activities.

Ecclesiastically, the churches have made great advance, especially the older groups. They have freed themselves from much of the old missionary paternalism and have made great progress in self-government, support, and propagation. Many are now independent of their founding mission boards and have become national and autonomous denominations.

Institutionally, the progress has been notable. Almost all of the larger groups have their own seminaries or Bible institutes for the preparation of pastors and lay workers. In 1968 in Central America there were five seminaries and nine Bible institutes with 616 students.[16] Around 1965 the Presbyterian Seminary of Retalhuleu, Guatemala, initiated a method of theological studies by extension, a movement that has extended throughout all of Latin America and has placed the study of theology within the reach of thousands who otherwise would be unable to do such studies.

In 1974 there were eight evangelical radio stations in Central America: TGNA, TGVE, and TGBA in Guatemala, YSHQ in El Salvador, HRVC in Honduras, YNOL in Nicaragua, TIFC in Costa Rica, and HOXO in Panama.

Evangelicals have also stood out in their educational and social work. They have primary and secondary schools in every country. These are more numerous in countries with a high percentage of illiteracy. Some of the secondary schools enjoy high esteem because of the exceptional quality of their instruction.

Evangelicals also excel in their literacy efforts. The emphasis on Bible reading has spurred the desire to learn to read. In Costa Rica, under the direction of an exiled Cuban Methodist, Justo L. González, evangelicals organized one of the largest literacy campaigns in modern times in Latin America. Its method is based on Laubach's system and is called *"Alfalit."*

In Guatemala, Honduras, Nicaragua, and Costa Rica the evangelicals have built hospitals. In Costa Rica, Honduras, El Salvador, and Nicaragua there are evangelical orphanages, and in Costa Rica a home for the elderly and various day care centers.

Also in Costa Rica the evangelicals organized a unique form of social service called "Good Will Caravans." A caravan is made up of a team of doctors, dentists, nurses, agronomists, "Alfalit" personnel, specialists in Christian education, evangelists, and so forth. Caravans go to places where there have been tragedies, such as floods and earthquakes, and to regions remote from medical, social, and religious attention. The caravan spends a period of time in the locality, rendering a multiple type of service that has been highly approved and praised by the local population as well as by civil authorities. Unfortunately, toward the end of the decade of 1970, this movement was losing its original character. Time and space will not permit me to describe in detail many other evangelical activities—the Salvation Army, rural centers, the distribution of Scriptures by the Gideons, university groups, youth camps, and child evangelism.

Some Present Problems

At the present, evangelicalism has its problems, but they differ from the former ones. It suffers little persecution from the Church of Rome, but instead is experiencing some of the same difficulties as the ancient church, such as increasing materialism and religious indifference.

Some churches have lost their "first love" (Rev. 2:4). Many evangelicals of the second and third generation have neither the enthusiasm nor the heroism that characterized their parents or grandparents. The number of persons who are no more than nominal evangelicals is increasing. To them social and secular interests are more important than the spiritual.

The "Protestant Ethic" has caused many to rise above their poverty and lack of culture. But added material and cultural blessings have sometimes proved what was said by the monk Caeser Heisterback (1180–1240): "Religion brought riches and riches destroyed religion."

Related to the above is the beginning of a relaxation of the puritan morals that characterized the early evangelicals. Scruples against cinema attendance have all but disappeared. Opposition to the use of alcoholic beverages still exists but less than before, especially in the use of wine. Divorce among evangelicals is on the increase and every now and then one hears of an evangelical alcoholic. In the early days ecclesiastical discipline was practiced strictly but today it is losing its ancient vigor.

In the decade of 1970 there arose a new type of discord. The great majority of the Central American evangelicals have been conservative in their theology, some even hyper-conservative. The Fundamentalist-Modernist controversy that shook North American Protestantism in the 1920s and 1930s affected Central America very little. However, at the beginning of the 1970s a polarization developed that transcended denominational divisions. At one extreme was a theology that emphasized the secular, provoked, perhaps, by the lack of social concern and a pseudo-pietistic disinterest in politics on the part of many evangelicals. It was particularly popular among university and seminary students.

Some in their enthusiasm for social justice rejected or looked down upon the traditional emphasis on personal evangelism, together with Christian piety and worship, and accepted the so-called "Theology of Liberation" with its Marxist orientation. According to this theology, the goal of Christianity should not be so much the redemption of the individual as the redemption of society. Following Marx, it holds that a renewed society will produce a new person, a thesis completely contrary to the teaching of classical evangelicalism. Furthermore, the "liberation" it proclaims has a character more political and economic than moral and spiritual. Its followers are a small but enthusiastic and vociferous group and constitute an intellectual elite.

At the opposite pole of this mode of thought there arose what one might call a "super" or "hyper-spiritualized" gospel. Pentecostalism, during the first years of its history in Central America, existed as a movement within evangelicalism, but clearly distinct and quasi-sectarian. In recent years, however, Pentecostalism has penetrated historic evangelicalism to form a movement called "renovation" or "neo-Pentecostalism." Its emphasis is altogether contrary to the secular gospel. Its adherents pursue the emotional and ecstatic: spiritual experiences, speaking in tongues, "prophesying," and casting out demons. Worship services, where they are predominant, are characterized by the singing of choruses, some of the "rock" type and others mystical (and usually lacking in real theological content or musical merit), accompanied by guitars and hand clapping.

Neo-Pentecostalism has become very popular in many evangelical churches, much more so than the Theology of Liberation. This polarization has been divisive. The leaders at both poles conceive of themselves as revolutionaries, social or spiritual. One group criticizes the traditional church for being too heavenly and not sufficiently earthy. The other would make the opposite accusation and accuse it of not being sufficiently attentive to the work of the Holy Spirit today. The two groups emphasize important aspects of the Christian faith but overemphasize their own points of view to the neglect of other aspects of the faith, and often their leaders and followers reveal a sectarian spirit and superiority complex.

In spite of the problems, however, the church goes forward, epitomized in a chorus popular among Central American evangelicals: *"En las luchas, en las pruebas la iglesia sigue caminando"* ("In the midst of struggles and trials the [evangelical] church marches on").

APPENDIX

Protestantism in Central America Since 1975

The original Spanish edition of this work was completed in 1975. This appendix is an attempt to update the story of Protestantism in Central America since that time.

Guatemala

Central America has always been a land of political and social turmoil (with the notable exception of Costa Rica) but in recent years this condition has augmented alarmingly. Nevertheless, the evangelical movement has grown more rapidly than ever. Since 1967 the annual growth rate of the Protestant community has been 10.5 percent—with the result that by 1980 there were approximately 2,316,600 adherents in a total population of 21,000,000. (It should always be remembered that in Latin America the evangelical community is reckoned to be three times the number of baptized members.)

The country that stands out most in Protestant growth is Guatemala, in spite of its suffering from chronic political turmoil. The cause for the turbulence in this country is not defined as ideologically as in El Salvador and Nicaragua; rather, it seems to originate in personal power struggles. But the tendency to polarization right and left is not lacking.

Notwithstanding, the numerical growth of the evangelicals has been phenomenal. In 1950 the Protestant community constituted only 2.8 percent of the Guatemalan populace. In 1981 it was 20 percent (or 1,400,000),[1] the highest percentage in any of the Latin American countries.

Guatemalan Protestantism is characterized by its extremely atomized condition. In 1978 there were 198 denominations operating in the country, although 23 accounted for 89 percent of the church membership. As in other countries, Pentecostalism has come to dominate the scene. In 1935 only 3 percent of the evangelicals were Pentecostal but by 1978 the percentage had risen to 58.2.[2]

Denominations with the largest membership are the Prince of Peace Church (Pentecostal), the Association of Central American Evangelical Churches (non-Pentecostal), Assemblies of God, Church of God (Cleveland, Tenn.), Seventh-day Adventists, National Presbyterian, and the Plymouth Brethren.[3]

Work among the Indians, who constitute 60 percent of the population of Guatemala, continues to be outstanding. According to a 1973 survey, approximately 36 percent of the Protestants in the country

were Mayan Indians. The Indian percentage undoubtedly would be higher if statistics were available from
the many other tribes.[4]

In March of 1982 it appeared that evangelicals
had achieved a notable triumph when General Efraín
Ríos Montt became president of the country in the
Guatemalan army's coup d'etat. Ríos Montt was an
elder in an evangelical charismatic group, "The Church
of the Word," that had begun a ministry in Guatemala
after the earthquake of 1976. Indicative of his evangelical fervor was the fact that he did not accept the
appointment until he had received approval from his
fellow elders.[5] However, the triumph was short-lived: in
August of the following year, the army demoted him
and named another general to take his place.[6]

The year 1982 was important for another reason:
it was the hundredth anniversary of the birth of the
evangelical cause in Guatemala (see pp. 29ff.). The
crowning event of the year was a meeting held on the
Campo Marte military field. The audience, estimated
at 350,000 to 700,000, was by far the largest evangelical gathering in the history of Latin America. It clearly
revealed the strength of evangelicalism in Guatemala.
The main speaker was the Argentinian evangelist Luis
Palaü. Following Palaü, President Ríos Montt gave a
message and led the huge audience in a prayer for the
welfare of the country.[7]

Belize

This small British colony, with a population of
only 146,000 (1981), achieved independence in 1981. It

continues to be principally Protestant, with a growing Catholic percentage. By 1980, 54.4 percent of the population was Protestant and 43 percent Roman Catholic. However, "nominal Christianity characterizes most people of Belize." Anglicans account for 46.5 percent of the Protestant community, Seventh-day Adventists for 24.3 percent, and Pentecostals for 16.2 percent. Pentecostals did not begin work in Belize until 1960, but they have progressed notably, from 500 in said year to 12,000 in 1978.[8]

Honduras

Evangelicalism has progressed in Honduras during recent years but not as notably as in the other republics, in spite of the relative stability the country has enjoyed. In 1965, 2.2 percent of the population was Protestant but by 1980 it had increased to 8 percent, with a community of 231,000. Between these two dates the annual increase was 13.4 percent while the general population growth was only 3.5 percent. The largest groups are the Seventh-day Adventists, Plymouth Brethren, and Moravians. The Pentecostals of Honduras constitute the lowest percentage in the evangelical community among the Central American republics, only 39 percent, while in Guatemala they compose 52.1 percent of the community and in El Salvador, 66 percent.

Turmoiled conditions in the neighboring republics have caused the influx of thousands of refugees. In the west they have poured in from El Salvador and in the east from Nicaragua. Most of the latter were Miskito Indians, among whom the Moravian faith predominates. The fleeing of the Miskitos was due to the ill treatment received from the Sandinista government. Fortunately they fled into territory where there were others of their tribe and where the Moravian Church was strong.

Ecumenical efforts have had little success in Honduras. An Evangelical Alliance, organized in 1959, started well but later weakened. However, in 1974, after the disastrous hurricane "Fifi," an Evangelical Committee for relief and Development (CEDEN) was organized and many preferred to cooperate with it than with the Alliance. In 1980 it had about thirty member organizations. Together with World Vision it has been facing the refugee problem.[9]

El Salvador

In recent years violent reaction against chronic social injustice has characterized the history of this small, overpopulated country, whose wealth in great part for decades has been in the hands of fourteen families. Thousands have been killed in the struggle between the guerrilla leftist bands and the rightist elements. Of late the government has taken steps to confiscate huge holdings and distribute the lands among the poor—but the effort seems to be tardy and the *guerrilleros* are not satisfied. In this struggle it is notable that the Church of Rome, once aligned with the landed aristocracy, has taken a strong stand for the poor and for human rights. Since 1977 eleven priests, Archbishop Romero, and four Catholic women missionaries from the USA have been killed in the escalating violence.[10]

In spite of the social unrest the Protestant community grew at the rate of 11.3 percent annually during the 1970s compared with 6.9 percent in the 1960s. The Pentecostals continue to be the largest contingent, 67.7 percent in 1978, while the non-Pentecostal evangelicals constituted only 15.3 percent of the community, not much more than the Seventh-day Adventists (13.9 percent). In 1980 the total Protestant community of El Salvador was 334,000 or 6.9 percent of the entire population.

Ecumenism has also been weak in El Salvador, due perhaps to the high percentage of Pentecostals. However, in 1979, in view of the national tragedy, the "Evangelical Salvadoran Committee for Relief and Development" (CESAD) was organized, patterned after similar agencies in Central America. The work of CESAD has been admirably seconded by that of World Vision.[11]

Nicaragua

Nicaragua is the republic most affected by political and social upheaval. In El Salvador the struggle between right and left continues, but in Nicaragua the leftists have taken over.

The present upheaval began when the dictatorial regime of the Somoza family (1933–79) was overthrown by the Sandinista *guerrilleros*. At first the revolution was a popular cause, given the heavy-handed, arbitrary and unjust forty-six-year rule of the Somozas. The evangelical attitude toward the revolution varied. Many young people embraced it, while some of the older people, fearing political turmoil or holding to the doctrine of passive obedience to the "powers that be," abstained from opposing the Somoza regime.

However, the founding of the "Evangelical Committee for Aid and Development" (CEPAD) affected greatly the relations between the evangelicals and the Sandinistas. Established after the terrible earthquake of 1972, in 1979 CEPAD was helping the victims of Somoza barbarities. When the Sandinistas took over the government, CEPAD cooperated with the revolutionaries in various social projects and because of many common aims became friendly with the new government. By 1982 CEPAD represented 80 percent of the evangelicals in the country.[12]

The Sandinistas have granted full religious liberty, and the evangelical cause continues to progress. Since the Sandinistas took power in 1979 the distribution of Bibles has increased fivefold and of New Testaments ninefold, due largely to the government's literacy program.[13]

However, the Sandinistas' veer to the left and their association with Cuba and Russia could not but affect the attitude of many. The growing animosity to the USA has obliged some missionaries to leave the country. There have been clashes between Sandinistas and evangelicals, yet CEPAD continues to support the regime, at the same time defending the evangelicals from unjust criticism and false charges.[14]

The blackest spot on the scene of the relations between evangelicals and the revolutionary government has been the treatment of the Miskito Indians of the north Atlantic coast. The Miskitos have lived in practical isolation from the rest of Nicaragua, although many of them, perhaps the majority, have accepted the Moravian faith. Somoza and his predecessors left them in peace in their isolation. However, the Sandinistas tried to impose on the Indians their social ideas and plans. The Miskitos rebelled and began to sympathize with the counterrevolutionaries. This brought cruel and bloody revenge from the Sandinistas, who burned many of their villages and attempted to march them into the interior and make it impossible for them to help the counterrevolutionaries. Many of the Indians were able to flee, most going to southeastern Honduras where other members of their tribe live.[15] By August 1982 there were 12,000 Nicaraguan Indians in Honduras.[16] One refugee in Costa Rica reported that on capturing a village the Sandinistas would take over the church and convert it into a military base and that they would burn the Bibles and torture the pastor.[17]

Still, the Sandinistas continue to grant religious freedom to all save those who oppose the regime, which is the "unpardonable sin." It would appear that if the revolutionary government continues to advance Marxist philosophy, the condition of Christians in Nicaragua will become similar to that in Cuba or even Russia.

In the midst of this, the Nicaraguan Protestant population increased from 4 percent of the population in 1950 to 12 percent in 1980. From 1966 to 1980 the annual increase was 12.5 percent. In the latter year the Protestant adherents numbered 281,000.[18] It is not yet clear as to what the final effects of Sandinismo will be on numerical growth.

Costa Rica

Costa Rica continues to be an island of freedom, democracy, and nonviolent social reform. In light of what has happened in Guatemala, El Salvador, and Nicaragua, she stands out more than ever in this regard.

In recent years the growth of the evangelicals has been 11 percent annually. By 1981 the community had reached 181,000 or 8 percent of the population, but it was divided into sixty-five denominations and independent groups. Pentecostalism continues to be the fastest growing sector. In 1960 it composed 10 percent of the community but by 1978 it had increased to 45 percent.[19]

Friendly relations with the Roman Catholic Church have cooled, due largely to the aggressive conservatism of the new archbishop, Román Arrieta, and also undoubtedly to the imprudent conduct of some evangelicals. Nevertheless, in 1983 one Catholic seminary (Instituto Teológico de América Central) honored the 500th anniversary of the birth of Martin Luther with a week of lectures given mostly by Protestant speakers.[20]

Endnotes

Notes to Chapter I

1. *Encyclopedia Britannica* (1962), XII: 873; K. S. Latourette, *A History of the Expansion of Christianity* (New York: Harpers, 1943), 5:51.
2. *Encyclopedia Britannica* (1962), IV: 202.
3. A. H. Anderson, *Brief Sketch of British Honduras* (Belize: Government Printer, 1948), pp. 28, 29.
4. Hubert Herring, *A History of Latin America* (London: Jonathan Cape [1957]), p. 436; *Encyclopedia Britannica* IV: 202; XI: 712A; XV: 844A; J. Fred Rippy, *Historic Evolution of Spanish America* (New York: F. S. Crofts, 1947), pp. 397–409.
5. Stephen Caiger, *Honduras Ahoy* (London: S.P.C.K., 1949), p. 13.
6. *Ibid.*
7. *Ibid.*
8. *Ibid.*, pp. 13, 14.
9. Ernesto Chinchilla Aguilar, *La Inquisición en Guatemala* (Guatemala: Ministerio de Educación Pública, 1953), p. 7.
10. *Ibid.*, pp. 26, 27.

11. *Ibid.*, p. 314.

12. *Ibid.*, pp. 150–52.

13. Gonzalo Báez Camargo, *Protestantes enjuiciados por la Inquisición en Iberoamérica* (México: Casa Unida de Publicaciones, 1960), p. 39.

14. *Ibid.*, p. 56.

15. *Ibid.*

16. Chinchillar Aguilar, *op. cit.*, p. 153.

17. *Ibid.*

18. *Ibid.*, pp. 153, 154.

19. *Ibid.*, p. 154.

20. *Ibid.*, p. 47.

21. *Ibid.*, pp. 67, 69.

22. Báez Camargo, *op. cit.*, p. 35; Chinchilla Aguilar, *op. cit.*, pp. 64, 65, 157.

Notes to Chapter II

1. Lloyd Mecham, *Church and State in Latin America* (Chapel Hill: University of North Carolina Press, 1934), pp. 71, 72.

2. *Ibid.*, pp. 370, 371; Mary Holleran, *Church and State in Guatemala* (New York: Columbia University Press, 1949), p. 67.

3. Holleran, *Church and State*, p. 62.

4. *Ibid.*, pp. 65, 66.

5. *Ibid.*, p. 68.

6. Marco T. Zeledón, *Digesto constitucional de Costa Rica* (San José: Colegio de Abogados, 1946), p. 30.

7. L. F. Gonzáles, "El cafe hizo levantar con vertiginosa rapidez el nivel económico del país," *La Nación* (San José, Costa Rica), 16 December 1951, p. 44; "Necrología" [of William Le Lacheur], *Gaceta Oficial* (San José, Costa Rica), 8 August 1963, p. 3.

8. Carlos Monge, *Historia de Costa Rica* (San José: Imprenta Las Américas, 1956), p. 146.

9. Mecham, *op. cit.*, p. 286.

10. *Gaceta del Gobierno* (San José), 4 September 1852, pp. 1, 2.

11. Zeledón, *op. cit.*, p. 68.

12. Holleran, *op. cit.*, pp. 173, 174.

13. *Ibid.*, p. 177.

14. L. F. González, *La historia de la influencia extranjera en . . . Costa Rica* (San José: Imprenta Nacional, 1921), p. 85.

15. *Ibid.*, pp. 293, 309.

16. Moritz Wagner and Karl Scherzer, *La República de Costa Rica en Centro America*, trans. Jorge Lines (1856; San José: Lehmann, 1944), p. 139.

17. Wilton M. Nelson, *A History of Protestantism in Costa Rica* (Lucknow: Church Growth, 1963), pp. 25, 26.

18. *Revista de Costa Rica en el siglo XIX* (San José: Tipografia Nacional, 1902), pp. 32, 33.

19. Wagner and Scherzer, *op. cit.*, p. 119.

20. Nelson, *op. cit.*, pp. 52–56.

21. *Ibid.*, pp. 56–60.

22. *Ibid.*, p. 57.

23. *Ibid.*, p. 63.

24. Robert Cleghorne, *Short History of Baptist Work in British Honduras* (London: Kingsgate Press, 1939), p. 15.

25. Kenneth Grubb, *Religion in Central America* (London: World Dominion, 1937), p. 140.

26. *Ibid.*, p. 25.

27. *Ibid.*, pp. 25, 26; Kenneth Hamilton, *Meet Nicaragua* (Bethlehem: Commenius Press, 1939), p. 18; Thelma Good, "125 years of Moravian Missions in Bluefields" (Bluefields, 1974), pp. 3, 4.

28. *Directory and Statistics, Moravian Church in America, 1975.*

29. Wagner and Scherzer, *op. cit.*, p. 50.

30. E. R. Huck, "Fortyniners in Panama: Canal Prelude" in Huck and Mosely, *Militarists, Merchants and Missionaries* (Alabama: University Press, 1970), p. 56.

31. R. Heber Gooden, *The Work of the Episcopal Church in Panama, Columbia, Costa Rica, Nicaragua and the Canal Zone* (Ancon, 1954), p. 2.

32. K. S. Latourette, *A History of the Expansion of Christianity* (New York: Harpers, 1943), 5:51.

33. *Ibid.*, pp. 53, 54; Ernest Payne, *Freedom in Jamaica* (London: Carey Press, 1946), pp. 64–71.

34. *Forever Beginning* (Kingston: Methodist Church, 1960), p. 56.

35. Nelson, *op. cit.*, pp. 71, 76, 79.

36. Victor Sanabria, *Primera Vacante de la diócesis de San José* (San José: Lehmann, 1935), p. 313.

37. *Revista de Costa Rica en el siglo XIX, op. cit.*, p. 36. In the census taken during the nineteenth century the inhabitants were questioned as to their religion.

Notes to Chapter III

1. It should be pointed out that these two groups have modified their policy and presently have missionaries in Central America who are working among Latins. In recent years even North American Catholics have come to consider Latin America as a mission field. In 1973 forty-three percent of the Roman Catholic mission force was in Latin America (*Mission Handbook, 1973* [Washington: U. S. Catholic Mission Council], p. 38).

2. Henry O. Dwight, *The Centennial of the American Bible Society* (New York: Macmillan, 1916), pp. 56, 79, 80.

3. The principal features of the Lancasterian system were (1) the advanced pupils taught the beginners and (2) the reading text was the Bible. This system became very popular in Spanish America after the Independence and was promoted by Bolívar and San Martín. It required little personnel and rapidly taught children to read. See Juan Varetto, *Diego Thomson,* (Buenos Aires: Imprenta Evangélica, 1918). See also article on "Lancaster, Joseph" in *Encyclopedia Britannica.*

4. Henry Dunn, *Guatemala o las provincias unidas de Centro America durante 1827 y 1828,* trans. Ricardo de Léon (Guatemala, 1960), pp. 79, 88, 89; Mary Holleran, *Church and State in Guatemala* (New York: Columbia University Press, 1949), p. 120.

5. Juan Varetto, *Federico Crowe de Guatemala,*

(Buenos Aires: Junta Bautista de Publicaciones, 1940); Kenneth Grubb, *Religion in Central America* (London: World Dominion, 1937), p. 61; Edward Haymaker, "The Beginnings of the Evangelical Movement in Guatemala" (Guatemala, 1946), pp. 5–7.

6. Wilton M. Nelson, *A History of Protestantism in Costa Rica* (Lucknow: Church Growth, 1963), p. 108.

7. Dwight, *op. cit.*, pp. 220, 221.

8. Claudio Celada, *Un apóstol contemporáneo* (Buenos Aires: La Aurora, 1945).

9. Enrique Denzinger, *El magisterio de la Iglesia* (Barcelona: Herder, 1961), pp. 381, 382, 407.

10. Pablo Burgess, *Justo Rufino Barrios*, 2d ed. (Quetzaltenango: Noticiero Evangélico, 1946), p. 109.

11. *Historia de la obra evangélica presbiteriana en Guatemala* (Guatemala: Noticiero Evangélico [1957]), pp. 17–25; Burgess, *op. cit.*, pp. 196, 197.

12. Haymaker, *op. cit.*, p. 15.

13. *Historia de la obra evangélica . . .* , *op. cit.*, p. 21.

14. Grubb, *op. cit.*, p. 60.

15. Haymaker, *op. cit.*, p. 15.

16. *Historia de la obra evangélica . . .* , *op. cit.*, pp. 20, 21; Haymaker, *op. cit.*, p. 17.

17. Nelson, *op. cit.*, p. 113.

18. Mildred Spain, *And in Samaria* (Dallas: Central American Mission, 1954), pp. 7, 8.

19. Nelson, *op. cit.*, p. 116.

20. *The Central American Bulletin*, vol. I, no. 4 (1895), p. 2. This was the official organ of the Central American Mission. Hereafter, references to this magazine will use the abbreviation *CAB*.

21. Nelson, *op. cit.*, pp. 119–47.

22. Spain, *op. cit.*, pp. 56–65.

23. *CAB*, 15 April 1900, p. 28.

24. *CAB*, vol. I, no. 4 (1895), p. 5.

25. *CAB*, 15 April 1896, p. 4; 15 October 1897, p. 5.

26. *Ibid.*

27. Spain, *op. cit.*, pp. 108, 109.

28. *CAB*, 15 April 1897, p. 28

29. Spain, _op. cit._, pp. 60, 62.

30. _Ibid._, pp. 155, 156.

31. _Ibid._, p. 163.

32. _Ibid._, pp. 214–17.

33. Crubb, _op. cit._, p. 86.

34. Nelson, _op. cit._, pp. 137, 138.

35. Wesley Amundsen, _The Advent Message in Inter-America_ (Washington: Review and Herald [1947]), pp. 88, 90.

Notes to Chapter IV

1. Mildred Spain, _And in Samaria_ (Dallas: Central American Mission, 1954), pp. 317–19; K. G. Grubb, _Religion in Central America_ (London: World Dominion, 1937), pp. 64, 120.

2. Grubb, pp. 62, 120.

3. _Historia de la obra evangélica presbiteriana en Guatemala_ (Guatemala: Noticiero Evangélica [1957]), pp. 57, 89.

4. _Ibid._, pp. 29–39.

5. _Ibid._, p. 46; Grubb, _op. cit._, pp. 64, 69.

6. Grubb, pp. 64, 65, 120; Delong and Taylor, _Fifty Years of Nazarene Missions_ (Kansas City: Beacon Hill Press, 1956), 2:145–52.

7. Paul Enyart, _Friends in Central America_ (Pasadena: William Carey Library, 1970), pp. 48–51, 53.

8. _Ibid._, p. 56; Grubb, _op. cit._, p. 120.

9. Enyart, _op. cit._, pp. 110ff.

10. _Ibid._, p. 52; Grubb, _op. cit._ p. 124.

11. Grubb, pp. 76, 122.

12. Enyart, _op. cit._, pp. 21–23; _The Church of God in the Americas_ (Cleveland, Tenn.: Church of God, 1954), p. 22.

13. Cristóbal Ramírez, _Las Asambleas de Dios en El Salvador_ (Santa Ana [ca. 1971]), pp. 5–13.

14. Grubb, _op. cit._, p. 122.

15. _Ibid._, p. 126.

16. Charles L. White, _A Century of Faith_ (Philadelphia: Judson Press, 1932), pp. 202, 203.

17. Grace Hatler, _Land of the Lighthouse_ (Philadelphia: Judson Press, 1966), p. 18.

18. White, *op. cit.*, pp. 202, 203.

19. Grubb, *op. cit.*, pp. 77, 122; G. Pitt Beers, *Ministry to a Turbulent America* (Philadelphia: Judson Press, 1957), p. 146.

20. Arturo Parajón, *Veinte cinco años de labor bautista en Nicaragua* (Managua, 1942), p. 18.

21. *Ibid.*, pp. 11–27.

22. *Ibid.*, p. 28.

23. Grubb, *op. cit.*, p. 126.

24. Parajón, *op. cit.*, p. 71.

25. *Ibid.*, pp. 71–79.

26. *Ibid.*, pp. 80–86.

27. In distributing the territory, the Panama Congress took into account only the large, historic denominations, not the independent missions nor the small denominations, which had already begun work in Central America.

28. Oscar Cáceres, "Ensayo histórico parcial del movimiento evangélico de Honduras" (San José: Seminario Bíblico, 1966), pp. 23–25.

29. Jorge Jacobs, "Historia de la Iglesia Evangélica y Reformada en Honduras" (San Pedro Sula, 1967), pp. 4, 9.

30. *Ibid.*, pp. 4, 5.

31. Grubb, *op. cit.*, p. 124.

32. Derby and Ellis, *Latin America Lands in Focus* (New York: Methodist Church, 1961), p. 45.

33. Wilton M. Nelson, *A History of Protestantism in Costa Rica* (Lucknow: Church Growth, 1964), pp. 163–65.

34. Grubb, *op. cit.*, p. 130.

35. Nelson, *op. cit.*, p. 168.

36. *Ibid.*, pp. 172–75.

37. *Ibid.*, pp. 175–85.

38. *Ibid.*, pp. 185, 186.

39. *Ibid.*, p. 193.

40. It should be clarified that Seventh-day Adventists may be classified as Protestants but not as evangelicals properly speaking. The principal doctrine that separates them from evangelicals is "Sabbathism," the doctrine that Saturday is the true day of worship and the observance of Sunday is a custom of pagan origin and constitutes the "mark of the beast" (Rev. 13: 17, 18).

41. Wesley Amundsen, *The Advent Message in Inter-America* (Washington: Review and Herald [1947]), pp. 103, 157.

42. Grubb, *op. cit.*, pp. 120, 122, 124, 126, 128, 130.

43. *Eco Estudiantil*, 1955 (Alajuela: Colegio Vocacional, 1975), p. 6.

44. John Wilson, "Obra Morava en Nicaragua; transfondo y breve historia" (San José: Seminario Bíblico, 1975), p. 217.

Notes to Chapter V

1. Due to lack of space it has not been possible to illustrate nor document much said in this chapter.

2. *The Central American Bulletin*, November 1923, p. 20.

3. *Panama Congress, 1916* (New York: Missionary Education Movement, 1917), 3:479.

4. Kenneth Grubb, *Religion in Central America* (London: World Dominion, 1937), p. 117.

5. *Ibid.*, pp. 104, 130, 137.

Notes to Chapter VI

1. Read, Monterroso, and Johnson, *Latin American Church Growth* (Grand Rapids: Eerdmans, 1969) pp. 138–63.

2. *North American Protestant Ministries Overseas Directory*, 9th ed. (Monrovia: MARC, 1970), pp. 236, 238, 239, 243, 245, 262, 263, 265.

3. *Ibid.*, p. 3.

4. *U. S. Catholic Overseas Missionary Personnel* (Washington: Mission Secretariate, 1962), pp. v, ix. "U. S. Catholic Mission Fields Abroad" (pamphlet without pages or date; Washington: U. S. Catholic Mission Council).

5. Kenneth Grubb, *Religion in Central America* (London: World Dominion, 1937), p. 118.

6. Read, Monterroso, and Johnson, *op. cit.*, pp. 138–63.

7. "Directorio Geográfico de las Iglesias y Misiones Evangélicas de Costa Rica" (San José: IINDEF, 1974).

8. *Historia de la obra evangélica presbiteriana en Guatemala* (Guatemala: Noticiero Evangélico [1957]), p. 156.

9. *Ibid.*

10. *Ibid.*, pp. 156, 157; José G. Carrera, "Breve exposición histórica de la Iglesia Presbiteriana en Guatemala" (1967), p. 5.

11. W. Stanley Rycroft, *The National Councils and Federations of Churches in Latin America* (New York: CCLA, 1961), pp. 8–10.

12. Wilton M. Nelson, *A History of Protestantism in Costa Rica* (Lucknow: Church Growth, 1963), pp. 251–53.

13. *Time,* October 5, 1959.

14. *Latin America Evangelist,* September 1955, pp. 172–74.

15. Among them, the present writer.

16. *Directory of Theological Schools* (London: T. E. F., 1968), pp. 44–47.

Notes to Appendix

1. Clifton Holland, *World Christianity, Central America and the Caribbean* (Monrovia: MARC, 1981), pp. 12, 71.

2. *Ibid.*, p. 71.

3. *Ibid.*, p. 83.

4. *Ibid.*, pp. 71, 72.

5. *Christianity Today,* April 23, 1982, pp. 32, 33; *Time,* April 5, 1982.

6. *La Nación* (San José, Costa Rica), 10 August 1983, p. 14A.

7. *Christianity Today,* January 1, 1983, p. 32.

8. Holland, *op. cit.*, pp. 15–17.

9. *Ibid.*, pp. 85–101.

10. *Ibid.*, pp. 53, 54.

11. *Ibid.*, pp. 55–63.

12. "Why the Gospel Grows in Socialist Nicaragua," *Christianity Today,* April 8, 1983, pp. 34–42.

13. *Ibid.*
14. *Ibid.*
15. *Ibid.; Time,* March 1, 1982.
16. *La Nación* (San José, Costa Rica), 22 August 1982, p. 26A.
17. *Ibid.,* 24 June 1983, p. 6A
18. Holland, *op. cit.,* p. 107.
19. *Ibid.,* pp. 34, 35.
20. Among them was the author.